NEW DIRECTIONS FOR INSTITUTIONAL RESEARCH

J. Fredericks Volkwein, *State University of New York at Albany*
EDITOR-IN-CHIEF

Larry H. Litten, *Consortium on Financing Higher Education,
Cambridge, Massachusetts*
ASSOCIATE EDITOR

Campus Fact Books: Keeping Pace with New Institutional Needs and Challenges

Larry G. Jones
University of Georgia

EDITOR

Number 91, Fall 1996

JOSSEY-BASS PUBLISHERS
San Francisco

CAMPUS FACT BOOKS: KEEPING PACE WITH NEW INSTITUTIONAL NEEDS
AND CHALLENGES
Larry G. Jones (ed.)
New Directions for Institutional Research, no. 91
Volume XVIII, Number 3
J. Fredericks Volkwein, Editor-in-Chief

Copyright © 1996 by Jossey-Bass Inc., Publishers, 350 Sansome Street, San Francisco, CA 94104-1342.

Microfilm copies of issues and articles are available in 16mm and 35mm, as well as microfiche in 105mm, through University Microfilms Inc., 300 North Zeeb Road, Ann Arbor, Michigan 48106-1346.

ISSN 0271-0579   ISBN 0-7879-9900-8

NEW DIRECTIONS FOR INSTITUTIONAL RESEARCH is part of The Jossey-Bass Higher and Adult Education Series and is published quarterly by Jossey-Bass Inc., Publishers, 350 Sansome Street, San Francisco, California 94104-1342 (publication number USPS 098-830). Periodicals postage paid at San Francisco, California, and at additional mailing offices. POST-MASTER: Send address changes to New Directions for Institutional Research, Jossey-Bass Inc., Publishers, 350 Sansome Street, San Francisco, California 94104-1342.

SUBSCRIPTIONS cost $52.00 for individuals and $79.00 for institutions, agencies, and libraries.

EDITORIAL CORRESPONDENCE should be sent to J. Fredericks Volkwein, Institutional Research, Administration 241, State University of New York at Albany, Albany, NY 12222.

Photograph of the library by Michael Graves at San Juan Capistrano by Chad Slattery © 1984. All rights reserved.

Manufactured in the United States of America on Lyons Falls Pathfinder Tradebook. This paper is acid-free and 100 percent totally chlorine-free.

CONTENTS

Editor's Notes

Campus fact books, by one name or another (fact book, data digest, data almanac, data atlas, information digest, statistical profile, and so on) and in one form or another (bound volume, loose-leaf volume, pamphlet style, pocket-sized, single page fact sheet, electronic) have become, since the mid- to late 1950s, an integral part of the institutional research effort at many colleges and universities. The fact book, a generally available document containing a compilation of objective and reliable quantitative and qualitative data and information that can be used by a variety of publics to define and describe the mission, goals, programs, personnel, and organization of an institution, has also become on some campuses an institution of its own.

In many respects, the development of the fact book has paralleled the development of the institutional research effort, and in the minds of many, fact books are a direct result of institutional research and institutional research offices (Smith, 1980; Smith and Strickland, 1979; Leischuck, 1970; Howard and McWhorter, 1977; West, 1957). As institutional research and researchers have become more sophisticated, so have institutional fact books. The very early fact books, often produced using ditto or mimeograph masters, are in sharp contrast to those produced today using desktop publishing and electronic reporting. While less visible, equally dramatic changes have occurred in the ways in which fact book editors can access, retrieve, and customize the data to meet fact book reporting requirements, making the fact book not only easier to produce, but generally easier for the reader to use.

To some observers, among them the chapter authors of this issue, there is a concern that over time the changes made in fact books have been more cosmetic than substantive. That fact books contain basically the same information now that they did thirty years ago may say something about the foresight of the first editors, but it may also reflect a comfort with the status quo that prevents the fact book from keeping pace with new institutional reporting needs. Clearly our wish is that the fact book be as viable and valuable in the future as it is today and as it has been over the years. We hope this issue will contribute to the continued success of the campus fact book both as a service to institutions and as a reflection of institutional research and researchers. Fact books have come a long way since their beginnings, but with the opening of the information highway, the ever-increasing demands for information, and the dramatic challenges facing higher education, perhaps the trip has only just begun.

This issue is devoted to exploring ways in which the fact book can remain and grow as a significant institutional research report both in light of new reporting demands and opportunities and in response to new and increased demands and uses for institutional data and information from and by internal and external constituencies. It may well be, however, that the real significance of this issue rests with Marks's observation (Chapter Two) about the quintessence of the fact book as an institutional research report and the implicit relationship between the fact book, institutional research, and institutional research as a profession: an observation that I feel is confirmed in Chapter One where the historical context of the fact book is examined. To consider the purposes, uses, content, and structure of the fact book, as Marks and Endo do in their chapters, as well as the philosophical and technical foundations of the fact book, as all of the issue authors do in their chapters, is to examine institutional research and its practice. Just as the historical development of the fact book mirrors the development of institutional research, so too may the future of the fact book reflect the future of institutional research.

Nevertheless, the primary focus of this issue is to provide ideas and techniques that will be useful in the development, review, and evaluation of institutional fact books. Joseph Marks (Chapter Two) and Jean Endo (Chapter Three) speak to fact book purposes and content and James Thompson (Chapter Four) provides ideas on how to put it all together in a paper fact book, while Robert Daly and Dennis Viehland provide the same information for producing an electronic fact book (Chapter Five). My fact book bias, that is, that the fact book can and perhaps should be an institution's most valuable publication and the most valuable report produced by institutional researchers, is argued in Chapter Seven and documented in Chapter One. Ann Tomlinson (Chapter Six) describes strategies she has used to make the fact book an essential and integral part of her office's and her university's operation. Ultimately it will be left to you, the reader, to search for the implicit relationships between the fact book and institutional research and ability of both institutional research and the fact book to meet the needs of your institution: we hope this issue will help you carry forth that examination and discussion.

Larry G. Jones
Editor

References

Howard, R. D., and McWhorter, M. A. "Fact Books: A Tool for Intra-institutional Communication." Paper presented at the Southern Conference on Institutional Research, Atlanta, Ga., Oct. 1977.

Leischuck, G. S. "Communicating the Results of Institutional Research: The Production and Uses of the Fact Book." In P. S. Wright (ed.), *Institutional Research and Communications in Higher Education.* Tallahassee, Fla.: Association for Institutional Research, 1970.

Smith, G. "Systematic Information Sharing in Participative University Management." *Journal of Higher Education,* 1980, 51 (5), 519–526.

Smith, G., and Strickland, W. G. "Moving Live Information to the Constituencies." *Planning for Higher Education,* 1979, 8 (1), 28–32.

West, E. D. Unpublished memo to Coleman R. Griffith, Office of Statistical Information and Research. American Council on Education, Washington, D.C., July 17, 1957.

LARRY G. JONES is public service associate and associate professor in the Institute of Higher Education at the University of Georgia.

*The early development of the campus fact book parallels the
development of institutional research; the fact book, perhaps the most
visible of all institutional research reports, reflects much of the
accomplishment and status of institutional research as an integral part
and essential function of higher education.*

A Brief History of the Fact Book as an Institutional Research Report

Larry G. Jones

The campus fact book most likely had its roots in fact books first created by national and regional organizations that were designed to "make available statistical data in a convenient, understandable, and accurate manner" (Elliott, 1996). If not the first educational fact book, *Statistics of Land-Grant Colleges and Universities,* published by the U. S. Office of Education, may well qualify as the longest-running series of statistical data on students, degrees, faculty, and finances in higher education in the United States. The first report covered the 1867–68 year, the second the 1869–70 year, and then an annual report was published every year until 1963: the 1963 issue of *Statistics of Land-Grant Colleges and Universities,* which was also the last, was the 94th edition. Although it focused on the sixty-eight institutions created by the Morrill Act of 1862 and subsequent amendments, comparative summary data for all two- and four-year institutions in the United States were included in *Statistics of Land-Grant Colleges and Universities* when the data were available.

Expanding enrollments and concerns over the quality of educational data for state and regional planning in the mid-1950s prompted national and regional organizations and associations to examine the available data, with the general conclusion that "the available data are not sufficiently complete or analyzed to be easily applied in practical affairs" (Folger and Sugg, 1956, p. iii). The *Fact Book on Higher Education in the South,* compiled by John Folger and Redding Sugg, Jr., for the Southern Regional Education Board (SREB) in 1956, was a response to "the need for dependable information about higher education. . . . Not only educators and college administrators, but also the many nonacademic people who have responsibilities for the management of higher education, need information which they can use confidently. Legislators and college trustees are asking for information in comparable form so that they may understand their institutions in state, regional, and national perspectives" (p. iii).

The purpose of the SREB *Fact Book* was "not only to make current information freely available but to encourage the uniform reporting of data throughout the region" (p. iii), and the early SREB fact books focused on state and regional data obtained from institutions, state agencies, and federal offices and reports. In 1961, SREB's Commission on Goals for Higher Education in the South recommended that "if excellence is to have any meaning at all, it is a universal concept, and we must insist that Southern colleges and universities be measured against the same criteria of excellence which are applied everywhere" (Godwin, 1980). Since that time, the SREB fact books have highlighted national data and averages in addition to the SREB state and regional information and averages, as shown by Exhibit 1.1, taken from the 1994/1995 edition of the *SREB Fact Book* (Marks, 1996a, p. 109).

Exhibit 1.1. Sample Display of SREB State, Regional, and National Averages

Average Salaries and Salary Rankings of Full-Time Instructional Faculty at Public Four-Year Colleges and Universities[1]

	All Ranks Average Salary 1993-94	Percent Change		Inflation-Adjusted Percent Change[2]		Salary Ranking		
		1988-89 to 1993-94	1992-93 to 1993-94	1988-89 to 1993-94	1992-93 to 1993-94	1988-89	1992-93	1993-94
United States	$48,200	19.5	2.7	-1.3	0.0			
SREB States	44,487	17.4	2.7	-2.9	0.0			
SREB States as a Percent of the U.S.	92.3							
Alabama	42,194	18.0	4.2	-2.4	1.4	9	11	10
Arkansas	40,592	23.8	2.9	2.4	0.2	13	13	13
Florida	46,153	11.9	3.0	-7.5	0.3	2	3	4
Georgia	45,150	16.6	2.5	-3.6	-0.2	6	6	6
Kentucky	44,852	28.5	2.8	6.3	0.1	10	7	8
Louisiana	38,820	25.6	-2.0	3.8	-4.6	15	12	15
Maryland	47,242	15.1	-0.4	-4.8	-3.0	3	2	2
Mississippi	40,800	17.6	3.8	-2.8	1.1	11	14	12
North Carolina	46,284	17.9	3.6	-2.6	0.8	5	4	3
Oklahoma	41,336	20.6	2.1	-0.3	-0.6	12	10	11
South Carolina	42,504	15.9	0.6	-4.2	-2.0	8	9	9
Tennessee	44,972	19.9	6.4	-0.9	3.5	7	8	7
Texas	45,680	15.6	3.2	-4.4	0.5	4	5	5
Virginia	49,134	12.5	1.5	-7.0	-1.2	1	1	1
West Virginia	38,849	24.8	6.5	3.2	3.6	14	15	14

[1]SREB classifies four-year colleges and universities into six categories. See SREB Public Colleges and Universities by Category on page 157.

[2]1993-94 academic year base.

SOURCES: SREB-State Data Exchange 1988-89, 1992-93, and 1993-94; American Association of University Professors, unpublished data, 1989, 1993, 1994.

Source: Marks, 1996a, p. 109. Used by permission of the Southern Regional Education Board.

In 1963, SREB published its second fact book with the title *Statistics for the 60's: Higher Education in the South,* and in 1965 returned to the *Fact Book on Higher Education in the South* title for the third edition. Since 1968, the *SREB Fact Book on Higher Education* (*in the South* was dropped from the title in 1986) has been issued biennially. When new data become available between issues, a *SREB Fact Book Bulletin* is distributed with the updated information. SREB also maintains a round-the-clock data center providing on-line access to complete *Fact Book* databases, and late in 1996 will add Internet access. Further efforts to meet the *SREB Fact Book* purpose were initiated in 1994 and 1995 with the publication of a state summary report highlighting *Fact Book* data for each of the fifteen states participating in the SREB. Exhibit 1.2 is taken from *Georgia Highlights 1994/1995* (Marks, 1996b, p. 6) and illustrates the *SREB Fact Book* material focusing on faculty salaries in Georgia.

Although it is not clear that any institutional fact book is the direct result of having the *SREB Fact Book on Higher Education* as a model, it is clear that the Southern Regional Education Board did have a direct influence on institutional research in the South and nationally, not only with its data reporting, but also with its efforts in promoting data collection and use. SREB staff were early supporters of institutional research and during the period 1960–1967 cosponsored at least ten conferences on institutional research and particular institutional research topics (Godwin, 1968). In fact, according to L. Joseph Lins' brief history of the Association for Institutional Research (AIR), it was at the SREB Institute on Institutional Research in Tallahassee, Florida on July 14, 1960 that "the National Institutional Research Forum, the forerunner of the Association for Institutional Research, was conceived" (Lins, 1966, p. i).

It is not unlikely that fact books, as a means of reporting institutional data, were indirectly a topic of discussion at the workshops, conferences, and institutes sponsored by SREB. Schietinger (1968), writing in the preface to the proceedings of the 1967 Athens (Georgia) workshop on institutional research, noted that "the topic of data keeping and reporting was included on the program . . . to emphasize that the accumulation of organized factual material is prerequisite to the operation of institutional research activity on any campus" (p. v).

Under the guidance of E.F. Schietinger, SREB Director of Research, the Southern University Group (SUG 25) was formed in 1970, and institutional researchers from the twenty-five public doctoral-granting universities in the SREB states met to examine mutual data and institutional research issues, methods, and reporting techniques relevant to their institutions and the region. As word of the SUG meetings spread, and others who were eager to benefit from the discussions appealed to join the sessions, the Southern Conference on Institutional Research was formed as a means of including institutional researchers in the public and private institutions in the SREB region not eligible for SUG 25 membership but equally interested in the issues. In 1978, the Southern Conference on Institutional Research was reorganized as the Southern Association for Institutional Research.

Exhibit 1.2. Sample Display of SREB State Highlight Data

• Since 1974, the average faculty salary in the South
has fallen almost 2 percent when adjusted for
inflation, while the national average rose
3 percent.

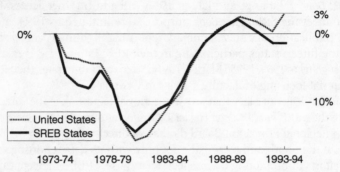

Change in Public Four-Year College Faculty Salaries Adjusted for Inflation

• Georgia has fallen from 2nd to 6th place among the
15 SREB states in terms of public four-year college
faculty salaries over the past 10 years.

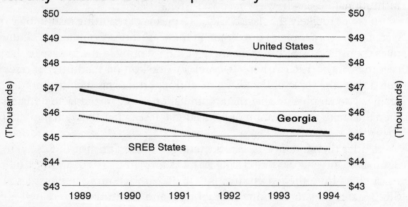

Public Four-Year College/University Faculty Salaries Adjusted for Inflation

Source: Marks, 1996b, p. 6. Used by permission of the Southern Regional Education Board.

Late in 1959, two other regional groups published and distributed fact books. The New England Board of Higher Education's (NEBHE) *Facts About New England Colleges and Universities* contained "information obtained through questionnaires on types of institutions, tuition and fees, enrollment, faculty and staff" (Sprague, 1960, p. 247). The Western Interstate Commission for Higher Education (WICHE) distributed the first five sections of its *Fact Book on Western Higher Education* in 1959 and mailed the remainder of the sections in 1960. Using questionnaire surveys to obtain the data, WICHE's *Fact Book* included information "specific to certain graduate and professional fields, student migration, capacity for potential growth of departments, areas of specialization within departments, number of degree candidates enrolled by department, and growth potential of certain departments, [based on existing] facilities and personnel" (Sprague, 1960, p. 247).

In July 1959, WICHE cosponsored with Stanford University "the first formal workshop on institutional research by colleges and universities in the Western region . . . attended by more than 130 college and university officials from all 13 of the Western states and from 12 states outside the West," and was reported to be a "major force in stimulating" more and better institutional self-study (Enarson, 1960, p. v). The 1959 conference, as well as one the following year cosponsored by the Center for the Study of Higher Education and the University of California–Berkeley, (focusing on the college student) and one in 1961, again at Stanford, (focusing on faculty studies), dealt directly with institutional studies, data collection, and analysis. That research undoubtedly provided fact book fodder. In fact, the relationship between the WICHE *Fact Book*, institutional research, and the WICHE-sponsored institutes on institutional research, is quite clear: "The *Fact Book on Western Higher Education* has been prepared primarily for those university and college officials who are concerned with 'institutional research,' that is, institutional self-study, and who frequently find the need for comparative data on other institutions and on nearby states" (Axt, 1960, p. iii).

The need for such regional data has been mentioned at a number of WICHE meetings and received particular attention at the Institute for College and University Administrators on Institutional Research, cosponsored by WICHE and Stanford University in July 1959 (Axt, 1960). It is also interesting to note that the WICHE *Fact Book* was "modeled after the most useful fact book of national data, published by Dr. Elmer D. West of the Office of Statistical Information and Research, American Council on Education" (p. iii).

At about the same time SREB was developing its fact book, Elmer D. West, in the Office of Statistical Information and Research (OSIR) at the American Council on Education, was proposing and preparing the *Fact Book on Higher Education* as his response to the deplorable condition of existing higher education data. According to West: "At that time, the existing quantifiable data about higher education were subject to widespread suspicion or even, in many cases, outright rejection. All too often data collected were not only inadequate but were not made available until the time of their usefulness was past. It had become increasingly apparent that data had to be improved in quality and in speed of dissemination. In addition, the data had to be presented in a clear and understandable form to be of maximum use to decision makers" (1984, p. vii).

In a lengthy memo, in which he addressed the question "what could—and what should OSIR do that would be of influence in the field of higher education in such a way that, in 1970, there would be less confusion and less bickering concerning the 'meaning' of 'higher education,' and more confidence in and comprehension of 'data' about higher education?" (1957, p. 1), West laid a philosophical and practical foundation for the fact book he created and edited, from 1958 to 1964, for the American Council on Education (ACE). Fundamental to the ACE *Fact Book*, it would seem, was West's idea that a new system of reporting higher education data was necessary and that the new system was predicated on outcomes that were as applicable to the raison d'etre of statistical reporting then as they are to fact books today (and, perhaps not so coincidentally, outcomes that matched the OSIR charter). Among these outcomes were the need to:

> provide . . . information about educational Statistics with emphasis on data relating to colleges and universities; analyze data . . . gathered by other agencies to appraise its usefulness for decision making by college and university administrators and to seek by all persuasive means to improve the precision and usefulness of such data; identify gaps in present statistical knowledge concerning higher education and encourage the cooperation of other interested agencies to seek and obtain such needed information; undertake studies designed to assist in the improvement of current procedures and practices in gathering and reporting statistics; make a limited number of studies of . . . special cogency and importance to higher education which [otherwise] are not likely to be undertaken; make studies from presently available statistics to bring into focus all available information relating to issues of special significance and importance; and publish and distribute . . . findings. [West, 1957, pp. 1–3, 6–7]

In the process of meeting these goals, OSIR sponsored a conference of college and university presidents, which "emphasized the magnitude of the gap between the quality of the data available to, and the data needed by, the chief administrative offices" (West, 1957, p. 1). More significantly, perhaps, OSIR also held a conference with institutional research personnel, "the first conference of such people," and it too confirmed the "gap between static and functional data" (p. 2). Clearly the goals outlined by West not only fit fact book purposes, but provide a rather good operational definition of institutional research as well. (Elmer D. West was awarded Distinguished Member status in the Association for Institutional Research in 1974, for his contribution to the development of the practice and profession of institutional research.)

In practical terms, West's two-part presentation of information, using the actual data and a diagram showing trends (Exhibit 1.3), is still in use in the ACE *Fact Book*. Although it first appeared in loose-leaf format as an incidental

Exhibit 1.3. West's Two-Part Presentation of Fact Book Information

174 College Work-Study Program: Awards and Recipients, Fiscal Years 1975–1986

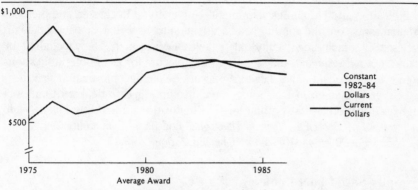

Fiscal Year	Total Awards (in $ millions)	Number of Recipients (in thousands)	Average Award (in current dollars)	Average Award (in constant 1982–84 dollars[a])
1975	$295.0	570.0	$518	$963
1976	436.1	696.7	626	1,100
1977	469.1	845.3	555	916
1978	488.5	852.5	573	879
1979	601.5	925.7	650	895
1980	660.2	819.1	806	978
1981	624.0	739.3	844	928
1982	614.9	720.1	854	885
1983	683.5	771.8	886	890
1984[b]	645.1	735.5	877	844
1985[b]	692.0	786.0	880	818
1986[b]	662.0	752.0	880	803

a   Converted to constant dollars using the CPI.

b   Estimate.

Sources

1   U.S. Department of Education, Office of Postsecondary Education, *Program Summary Book for 1985–86* (Washington: GPO, 1987), p. 100.

2   CES, *Digest of Education Statistics, 1987* (Washington: GPO, 1987), p. 30.

Source: Anderson, Carter, and Malizio, 1989, p. 232. Used by permission of the American Council on Education.

publication, the ACE *Fact Book* progressed to a quarterly and then an annual issue. In 1980 and 1981 it was published as the *Fact Book for Academic Administrators,* and returned as the *Fact Book on Higher Education* in 1984–85, 1986–87, and 1989–90. Early editions of the *Fact Book on Higher Education* (1958–1962) were distributed free, with funding from the Carnegie Corporation, to the president of every ACE member institution and organization and gave the publication wide national distribution and visibility (Elliott, 1996).

Other national fact books on higher education followed. The *Digest of Education Statistics,* covering education in the United States from kindergarten through graduate school, was issued in 1962 by the U.S. Office of Education, and the editors of the *Chronicle of Higher Education* began the *Almanac of Higher*

Education as a supplement in 1988 (it also appeared as a separate University of Chicago publication, 1989–1995). The *NEA 1994 Almanac of Higher Education,* a publication commissioned by the National Education Association (NEA), is produced by the Higher Education Program, Margaret S. Warner Graduate School of Education and Human Development, University of Rochester, and includes original essays on "the conditions of academic life" as well as statistical data on "key statistics, including [faculty] salary tables" (Wechsler, p. 5). By including the essays, the *NEA Almanac* may represent a departure for fact book publications from primarily quantitative data to significant qualitative information as well.

Several specialized fact books have also emerged to deal with national higher education issues, populations, or institutions, including *Public Negro Colleges: A Fact Book; Fact Book on Theological Education; Community College Fact Book;* and *Fact Book on Women in Higher Education.*

Campus-Based Fact Books

One of the first campus-based fact books, if not the first, was *Fact Book for the Florida State University,* produced by the FSU Office of Institutional Research and Service and published in June 1961. The foreword to the FSU *Fact Book* gives the motivation and purpose for the publication:

> During recent years many studies have been made concerning the Florida State University. These studies have resulted in routine reports which have been issued periodically by various University offices and special reports prepared by individuals and University agencies. Many of these studies have been made in response to requests: by University officers and agencies, by the Florida State Board of Control, by officers of the state government of Florida, by agencies of the federal government, by organizations such as the American Council on Education and the Research Division of the National Education Association, and by other individuals and agencies. The studies have examined a wide variety of aspects of the Florida State University.
>
> In view of the large number of studies completed and in response to a feeling of need that the essential findings of many of these studies be compiled into a single volume, the Office of Institutional Research and Service has prepared the text for this *Fact Book.*
>
> Inasmuch as this is a first effort at a publication of this kind, there may be errors and omission of items which should have been included. Comments and suggestions are invited to the end that subsequent editions of the *Fact Book* may meet more adequately the needs of those who constitute the professional staff of the Florida State University. [p. ii]

The table of contents for the FSU *Fact Book* carried the heading "A Fact Book to report FACTS AND FIGURES Pertaining to the FLORIDA STATE UNIVERSITY, Including:" and listed seven parts: History and Government; Organization and Administration; Enrollment Data; Student Abilities, Grades,

Fellowships, and Degrees Conferred; Faculty and Faculty Load; Financial Data; and Physical Facilities (Florida State University). The FSU Office of Academic Research and Planning, the successor of the Office of Institutional Research and Service, continues to publish the Florida State University *Fact Book*.

One very early institutional fact book is directly attributable to West's ACE *Fact Book on Higher Education*. In 1960–61, John Swanson was charged with the responsibility of coordinating the self-study process for accreditation at Auburn University. Finding that most of the required data and documentation were already available somewhere on campus, it is reported that Swanson realized he only needed to find a process to gather and report the data to be used, and remembering the ACE fact book, he developed the Auburn University fact book, *Facts and Figures,* in 1962 as the solution to his problem (Gerald Leischuck, telephone interview, June 1996). Perhaps it is more than coincidence that Swanson was at Florida State before he took the position at Auburn.

Another early fact book, a pocket-sized one, was produced at Foothill College (California). In 1961, at a conference on institutional research in the junior college sponsored by UCLA, President Calvin C. Flint reported that institutional research was one of the college's expressed objectives, including provision in the organizational chart for a full-time director of research. In anticipation of the director of research, a faculty research committee developed a list of the major items of information it thought should be "continually assembled" (Flint, 1962). The list reads like the table of contents of an institutional fact book. Although it was small, the first Foothill College fact book was produced in 1962.

Five years later, unaware of the Auburn fact book or of any other institutional fact book, but inspired by the ACE *Fact Book,* I produced my first fact book at Wittenberg University. Sharing the fact book at a show-and-tell at the AIR Institute in Minneapolis in the summer of 1968 with other researchers, it was clear that the idea of an institutional fact book was popular but untested. Knowing how quick institutional researchers are to copy, beg, borrow, or steal any good idea, it might be safe to say that many institutional fact books came directly from the ACE fact book idea or from someone who got the idea from West's work in the first place.

Historians and other researchers would be quick to point out, of course, that "attempts at integrating massive amounts of data into a coherent body of facts have been ongoing since the founding of American colleges and universities" using college catalogs, commencement programs, and other campus publications to provide information to prospective students, parents, alumni, legislators, and the public at large about their institutions (Eck, 1996, p. 1). The fact book set itself apart from these other publications, however, in purpose, in depth and breadth of institutional information, and in its use on and off campus (see Chapters Two, Three, Five, Six, and Seven). In the South, fact book development as the medium for institutional information was fostered by the Commission on Colleges of the Southern Association of Colleges and Schools (SACS)(1974), which promoted the use of a fact book as a part of the self-study process, including yearly updates for "application in long-range planning, grant proposals, and preparing news releases" (Smith and Strickland, 1979). When coupled with the SACS endorsement and the early institutional research efforts of SREB, one might assume that the early fact book models represented by the fact books of SREB, Florida State, and Auburn would have led to the rapid growth of fact books among southern institutions. A survey of the major public universities in the South suggests that did not happen, at least at these institutions, and that fact book development was probably more influenced by internal than external factors.

About fifteen years after publication of the first institutional fact book, Howard and McWhorter (1977) reported that 47 percent of the institutions responding to their survey on the production and use of fact books published one. It would seem, however, that most of the development in institutional fact books occurred during the 1970s. A search of the annual issues of the *Annotated Bibliography of Institutional Research,* 1966–67 through 1973–74, found the first listing of a fact book (*The University of Georgia Fact Book,* 1969, edited by Gary Stock and Nathan R. Keith, Jr.) in the 1969–70 issue. Other fact books listed in the AIR *Bibliography* included the *Fact Book of the University of South Florida,* 1970; *Fact Book 1970–71,* The University of Calgary; *Georgia State University Fact Book,* 1972–73, 1973–74, and 1974–75; and the *University of Alberta Data Book 1973–1974.* An analysis of the programs and proceedings of the annual AIR Forums, 1965–1976, found the first program sessions devoted to fact book themes in 1970. Jerry L. Kirks described efforts at Wayne State University to develop a six-year statistical survey to "summarize both graphically and by tables, pertinent data which could be used by people both inside and outside of the University" (Kirks, 1968, p. 52). Kirks described the "Six-Year Statistical Survey" in the context of a "statistical collection which can be affectionately referred to as the red book, or the blue book or the green book," that "every university or at least most universities have" (p. 52) presumably in reference to a fact book. The second fact book session at the 1970 Forum (the tenth annual) was Gerald S. Leischuck's paper "Communicating the Results of Institutional Research: The Production and Uses of the Fact Book," outlining a practical approach to the why and how of producing an institutional fact book (Leischuck, 1970).

The evidence suggests that although fact books weren't a topic of primary importance in the "formal" proceedings and publications of the AIR during the period, they were nonetheless being developed on campuses during the late sixties. In a 1971 AIR Forum workshop, Harry Bluhm, University of Utah, referred to the fact book, or as it was called at his institution, the *Statistical Summaries,* as "a major publication of many institutional research offices" (Bluhm, 1971, p. 180), and that statement, coupled with Kirks' (p. 52) inference that "every university, or at least most of them" had a fact-book-like report, suggests that institutions were producing fact books, even though they were going unheralded in the profession, the professional literature, and at professional conferences. Perhaps the lack of recognition for the development of the fact book during this period was a reflection of what was considered institutional research. In a 1968 monograph, *Junior College Institutional Research: The State of the Art,* John Roueche and John Boggs wrote: "It is true that . . . colleges often compile elaborate, well-bound data reports—but typically these data have little significance or value in or out of the college. The mere compilation of data does not constitute institutional research. Data collection may be construed as research activity if the data are being gathered 'to provide the answers to the right questions.' But questions and data must be coordinated in the research design" (1968, p. 50).

Although Roueche and Boggs may not have been referring directly to the fact book, their notion that compiling data was not institutional research may have been shared by others. In the same chapter, however, Roueche and Boggs suggest that "institutional research may be called successful if it has some effect on institutional practice," and that "research that does not change institutional practice is ineffective and fails" (p. 49). I would argue, using that criteria, that fact books have proven to be both successful institutional research and effective research. Perhaps we have since come to realize the contribution of the institutional fact book in connecting institutional data to institutional issues; in providing answers to significant institutional questions; and in leading to change in institutional policy and practice.

During the late sixties and early seventies, so many institutions and institutional researchers were so busy doing the research that would produce data for a fact book that few had time to either do a fact book or tell others about how to do one: lack of fact-book-centered presentations at conferences, workshops, and institutes during the period may reflect nothing more than that fact alone, according to one conference program planner who was active at that time (Edith Carter, telephone interview, June 1996).

Of those who were not publishing a fact book in 1977, "lack of manpower," "no perceived need," and "lack of funds" were the most frequently given reasons, in that order, for not doing so (Howard and McWhorter, 1977). Although there are few offices of institutional research that would claim they have adequate staff to do all they would like to do, or is expected of them, two solutions to the lack of manpower issue as it relates to fact book production may have surfaced since the Howard and McWhorter study. The first is the realization that Leischuck's (1970) argument that the fact book is a labor-saving device was in fact true, and that time spent developing a fact book was time saved later by having fact book answers to fact book type questions, as many institutional researchers will testify (see Chapter Six for one testimonial). The second manpower solution, and probably the more important, resulted from the increased accessibility to institutional data through the use of the computer. Quite simply, it has become easier with each passing year for institutions to access more and more data, and often with fewer people (either by choice or necessity) to do so.

The lack of perceived need for a fact book is not so easily explained or understood, but it is easier to find arguments for a fact book in the literature than it is to find arguments against a fact book: in fact, none were found. Even

Jim Montgomery's (1967) use of the University of Tennessee's fact book as an illustration of a descriptive study that, after six months of preparation, would be "carefully filed and forgotten" (p. 7) was not so much a condemnation of the fact book or the work it took to complete it as it was a comment on the use of institutional research at the time, or perhaps even a comment on compiled research. In fact, Montgomery later referred to the fact book as a "useful form of summary data" in the preparation of analytic and summary reports (Saupe and Montgomery, 1970, p. 6). There persist, however, stories on my campus about how reluctant some administrators are to make available data about the institution that might be used to challenge programs and policies, and I have heard others suggest that similar feelings are found on their campuses, particularly during discussions of fact book distribution. There have even been a few reports of institutional researchers who are reluctant to publish fact books for fear of losing control of the data.

It might be said at this point that if data or information is power, then in terms of the Total Quality Management movement supported by many in higher education these days, sharing of data through institutional fact books is an important way of *empowering*. Robert Daly, in discussions about his chapter and other chapters in this volume, suggested that the *intranet*, the internal distribution of fact book data, may be a more pressing institutional issue and may hold more potential for productive and exciting electronic fact books than the Internet. Not only does he view the intranet as politically astute for many institutions, he views it as the productive foundation of the dynamic or interactive fact book.

As previously mentioned, there has been and continues to be the fear that with the sharing of data and information comes the loss of power or control. Perhaps the best illustration of this fear came with the first influx of personal computers and shared data and the concern of many institutional researchers that it would mean the loss of institutional research positions and offices. Even in retrospect that seems far-fetched, but many in the field at that time will remember those discussions. Unfortunately, there still are examples of institutions withholding or withdrawing data from general use and circulation either for fear of losing control or power or simply to avoid answering the questions that the data may raise. One of the authors of this issue recently had to shut down much of his electronic fact book for these very reasons.

To the contrary, however, the previously mentioned encouragement of a regional accrediting agency (Folger and Sugg, 1956; Smith and Strickland, 1979), and the papers and articles by West (1957; 1983); Leischuck (1970); Fincher and McCord (1973); Nichols, Howard, and Sharp (1987); Smith (1980); and Howard and McWhorter (1977) suggest that the perceived need for a fact book has been consistently positive. More to the point is the current perception that institutional fact books are now more the rule than the exception: that, unlike in 1977, more institutions are publishing fact books in 1996 than are not. As one higher education observer and frequent visitor to a significant number of public and private two- and four-year institutions reports, it is rare to find a college or university that does not have a fact book. (Gerald Lord, telephone interview, June 1996).

The Howard and McWhorter (1977) study also indicated that lack of funds was both a reason for not producing a fact book and one of the most common problems faced when publishing one. It is unlikely that the cost of printing a fact book is less today than it was in 1977 or that it will be so in the future (at one institution, the cost of printing the fact book went from $1.56 per copy to $4.78, a 326 percent increase over a 21-year period). Clearly, the expense of producing a fact book could become, if it is not already, a major concern for those institutions now publishing them or considering it.

Closely tied to printing costs is the issue of fact book distribution. Typically, administrators (the president, vice presidents, and deans) automatically receive a fact book, and, somewhat less often, department chairs are included among that group. Less likely to automatically get a copy of the institution's fact book are the faculty, state agencies, and trustees. Generally speaking, all that request a fact book are given one, but automatic distribution seems to be limited at most institutions (Howard and McWhorter, 1977).

One of the most commonly proposed current solutions to the problem of fact book printing costs is an electronic fact book (see Chapter Five in this volume; Nichols, Howard, and Sharp, 1987, p. 109). Although electronic fact books are unlikely, in the near future, to completely eliminate the need for print editions (see Chapters Five and Six in this volume; Gusler, 1988), electronic transmission of the data and print-on-demand options are seen as viable alternatives.

One of the first electronic fact books was produced by Allan MacDougall at Southwestern College (1978) using Execucom's IFPS. Unlike the paper-based fact book, which took about eight years to capture the attention of institutional researchers by way of a formal presentation, the first electronic fact book AIR Forum session appeared in 1979, one year after the first report of an electronic fact book. "Automating the President's Factbook (sic)," a workshop given by Jon S. Hesseldenz of the University of Kentucky, was presented at the San Diego Forum, and dealt with "techniques to computerize the information usually found in the factbook (sic) (enrollment statistics, financial information, degrees granted, etc.)" (Staskey, 1979, p. 47). In contrast, the first AIR Forum workshop on paper fact books, "Developing an Institutional Fact Book," was held in 1981 (Association for Institutional Research, 1981, p. 40), twenty years after the first fact book appeared in print. The Developing an Institutional Fact Book workshop was repeated at the 1982 Forum, which may have been an indication of interest in the topic at the time (p. 43).

Currently, there are at least forty-six institutions that have electronic fact books using World Wide Web and Gopher technologies listed on a registry maintained by Tod Massa, Willamette University, and that listing is known to be incomplete: fact books available on the Internet at Web sites will undoubtedly increase those statistics dramatically in the near future. No institution has been identified that has only an electronic fact book available to users, although Robert Daly, University of California-Irvine, experimented with that approach and discovered that "sometimes it is easier to have a printed piece of paper" (Robert Daly, personal correspondence, 1996). Interest in electronic fact books is keen, as witnessed by the AIR Electronic Fact Book Special Interest Group that has been meeting at AIR Forums since 1989. Unfortunately, electronic fact books have their own set of associated problems, among them cost, in both human and technological terms, and consequently may not yet have made their full impact on the production of campus-based fact books. There is no question, however, that fact books of the future will be electronically shaped. Whereas the first electronic fact books were generally just an "electronic reproduction of a printed page" (see Chapter Five in this volume), dynamic electronic fact books provide for interactive exchange and even customized development of fact book data and pages.

Specialized Fact Books

Fact books have spawned a number of spin-offs over the years, some that act as companion pieces, some as replacements or substitutes, some as separate fact-book-like publications. Marks (Chapter Two), Endo (Chapter Three), and Tomlinson (Chapter Six) recognize in their chapters the need for and use of special or issue-oriented fact books to focus attention on topics of particular interest and concern to an institution or specific constituent group. North Carolina State, for several years, published three fact books (statistical profiles) focusing on students, staff, and finances as separate issues, and as previously mentioned, SREB publishes separate reports for each of its member states using fact book data. In these cases the primary purpose of the specialized fact book is to highlight or feature a particular issue or concern at a level of detail beyond the scope of a regular fact book.

One of the more common types of special fact books is the pocket-sized or mini fact book, a version small enough to carry around in comfort (Chapter Six in this volume; Holmes, 1976, p. 10). Although limited, the condensed version generally carries summaries of enrollment, tuition and fees, faculty and staff, facilities, degrees awarded, finances, and administrative contacts. Not only are the mini fact books less costly to print, they are much easier to carry and to distribute to the public. Fact sheets, one-page summaries of fact book information (or simply pages from the fact book), are often used in the same way and for the same reasons as the mini fact books (Chapter Six). Fact book pamphlets are something between the mini fact books and the fact sheets, but again are condensed in data volume and designed for broader distribution at less cost than a regular fact book (Chapter Six). In some cases the fact sheets are three-hole-punched for collecting in a notebook. Of course, loose-leaf fact books are not uncommon, facilitating the addition of new data, correction or updating of old data, or even distribution of certain data to selected individuals or offices. The primary purpose of the mini fact book, fact book pamphlet, and fact book sheet as fact book variations seems to be public relations.

At the University of Maryland, an easel approach was used to present fact book data to selected administrators. Summaries of admissions, enrollment, faculty and staff, faculty workload and salaries, finances, tuition/fees, grades, degrees, financial aid, retention, and graduation and other fact-book-type data were prepared for desktop easels for easy data retrieval and display. Although the summaries are now maintained in loose-leaf notebooks, the purpose of the reference handbooks was to provide for a more dynamic (one that could be easily changed) format as opposed to a static annual bound fact book volume (Daniel Thomas, personal correspondence, June 1996).

Fact Book Uses

Although fact books have taken on different sizes, shapes, and forms over the years, they continue to serve the same and generally similar functions for which they were first intended. Primary among these fact book functions is the use of the fact book as a data resource. In fact, it is clear from the developers of early fact books (West, 1974; Folger and Sugg, 1956; Leischuck, 1970; Howard and McWhorter, 1977) that one of the goals set for fact books was to gather in one place the relevant data required for decision making, planning, self-study, public relations, and communications, and in turn, each of those became a fact book purpose to one degree or another.

Data Resource. As a data resource, the fact book captures and summarizes most of the important current and historical data about the organization and operation of an institution and its component parts. But perhaps more important, the data it reports are reliable, consistent, uniform, comparable, and conform to generally accepted institutional or regional and national data definitions. By bringing together the essential data about an institution in one widely available source, the fact book manages to accomplish several other significant goals. It generally settles the issue of which data are correct or at least acceptable; it saves time and resources by eliminating the necessity of data searches every time a question is asked; and it provides the same information, in the same way, to every audience. It also provides the opportunity for an institution to highlight the information that makes it unique.

Decision Making. As a ready reference, the fact book provides, almost immediately, the base line data, trend data, and comparative figures often required for inquiry and analysis by decision makers, often without additional data manipulation. And, in the collegial setting, it is literally true that decision makers are spread across campus, occupying various positions with different levels of status. Smith and Strickland (1979, p. 29) noted that the shared decision-making environment of higher education was dependent on "trust and consensus building" and that "sharing the same common-core information about the institution with administrators, faculty, students, and governing bodies" was an important ingredient in the process. No small part of participating in the decision-making process is having the same basic information to consider.

Planning. As a planning document, the fact book often provides answers to questions like Where have we been?, Where are we now?, What will it take to get us where we want to go?, and How much headway did we make this year?

I once overheard a colleague say at the end of an AIR Forum session on planning that "[X institution's] fact book is our planning document: the president wants us to be like them, and it tells us what we have to do." Perhaps more to the point is that the fact book data helps everyone at an institution understand what the institution has become and can help identify those areas where more work needs to be done to fulfill its mission or achieve its goals.

Self-Study. The role of the fact book in self-study for institutional accreditation has already been noted (Leischuck, 1996; Smith and Strickland, 1979; Southern Association of Colleges and Schools, 1974). What may be overlooked is that the fact book not only serves the institution in the accreditation process, including the on-campus committees, but provides the visiting team members with additional data, information, and institutional perspectives that are invaluable (Grover Andrews, personal interview, June 1996; Gerald Lord, telephone interview, June 1996). Moreover, the fact book serves well as an indicator of areas that may need special institutional attention leading to or supporting internal self-studies of programs, policies, or procedures. While the Howard and McWhorter study did not find much use of the fact book in 1977 for evaluation studies, it might be assumed that the increased attention since that time on assessment, accountability, and institutional effectiveness has led to greater fact book use in related institutional self-study.

Public Relations. Public relations and related public information uses of the fact book seem to have been well served over the years (Howard and McWhorter, 1977; Gusler, 1988). Although there are those who argue that fact books whose primary purpose is public relations need to be developed accordingly, and in a somewhat different manner and format than fact books serving mainly as on-campus statistical references (Gusler 1988; Leischuck, 1970), it is possible that one fact book will serve both, or multiple purposes, or that mini fact books, fact sheets, or pamphlets can be developed to specifically meet public relations purposes. The fact book is, of course, an ideal way of describing the mission, programs, activities, and progress of the institution, both qualitatively and quantitatively, to both lay and professional publics, and it can be used to meet the public accountability concerns of legislatures, boards, and other constituents. It is an excellent medium for communication.

Communication. The last of this short list of uses that have been made of campus fact books is undoubtedly a part of each of the other uses mentioned. Early fact books were intended to communicate data and information, and that purpose has been met and expanded through electronic fact books and specialized fact books as well as by an expansion of the material fact books cover and an expansion of the readers served. The fact book has opened lines of communication with otherwise disparate groups, including faculty, students, administrators, and boards within an institution (Smith, 1980). And equally important, the fact book has helped communicate a sense of direction that is able "to link diverse groups into a mutual commitment toward advancement of the *total* institution" (p. 525). Implicitly and explicitly, the fact book also communicates what is important at and about the institution in a way that speeches, news releases, alumni magazines, newsletters, and campus newspapers cannot.

Institutional Research Report

In Chapter Two, Joseph Marks refers to the fact book as the "quintessential institutional research report—a work defining the essence of the profession, a work embodying the core principles, values, and skills." My guess is that few would argue that the fact book is the most visible example of institutional research reporting; that many would agree that the fact book is indeed a good example of institutional research reporting (*good* institutional research reporting); and that most would concur that the fact book does indeed "[embody] the core principles, values, and skills" of institutional research. Although there is clearly more to institutional research than just producing a fact book, there may be no other tangible evidence that so clearly and so simply demonstrates and "[defines] the essence of the [institutional research] profession" (see Chapters Two, Six, and Seven).

The historical development of the fact book into the quintessential institutional research report may in fact prove to be the most significant fact book legacy.

Quintessential Institutional Research Report

All institutional research reports serve one or more of six critical reporting objectives: (1) data transmission; (2) data preservation; (3) data interpretation; (4) issue identification; (5) issue resolution; and (6) evaluation. Fact books have been used to accomplish, directly and indirectly, and to one degree or another, all six of those institutional research reporting objectives.

Data Transmission. Fact books have probably gained most of their notoriety meeting the data transmission objective. Glynton Smith, an early fact book advocate and editor, defined the fact book as a source of "useful, objective, and reliable institutional data that provides a relatively concise overview of most facets of institutional operations" (Smith and Strickland, 1979, p. 28). According to Elliott (1996) "fact books became higher education's solution to assimilating, organizing, and regulating the vast amounts of data that computers generated in order to respond to internal and external requests for accurate information to inform decision making" (p. 1).

Two chapters in this issue deal directly with the data transmission role of the fact book. James Thompson's chapter deals with the very practical concerns of producing a fact book that is both readable and useable. As more than one discouraged institutional researcher has found, the message can be lost in the medium, and Thompson's chapter is a mini manual for putting together in technically correct ways institutional data that will not only convey the message but enhance the fact book medium as well. His chapter will give courage to the first-time fact book editor and will provide publication review guidelines for the seasoned fact book editor.

Robert Daly and Dennis Viehland's chapter on electronic fact books also deals in a very practical way with using the computer to transmit and distribute fact book data. Their chapter may in fact close the circle on the fact book and computer relationship. Early printed fact books were used to publish considerable amounts of institutional data generally available for the first time by virtue of emerging management information systems and mainframe computer technology. In their chapter, Daly and Viehland make the case for using the current computer technology for both generating the fact book data and electronically reporting it, creating in the process an interactive on-line fact book. It seems clear in this context that institutional research and the fact book are traveling the information highway together.

Data Preservation. With little fanfare, the fact book has become on many campuses the primary historical reference and resource for institutional data (Howard and McWhorter, 1977; Fincher and McCord, 1973). Generally thought of as a current publication, the fact book is often viewed as the yearbook of institutional data, highlighting the changes in various programs and statistics and documenting in measurable ways the institution's progress during the year. Along with the current-year data, data from previous years are often included for the purpose of comparison and trends, but just as often previous fact books must be used to find comparable data for previous years. As a result, complete collections of fact books are valued and jealously guarded on many campuses. Widely recognized as a resource document and reference for institutional data (Howard and McWhorter, 1977), the fact book is also viewed as a time saver for people and computers, because in it is collected and stored existing data from a variety of campus sources (Gerald Leischuck, telephone interview, June 1996). In this case, the fact book represents not only a quantitative history of the institution, but a record over time of institutional research as well.

Data Interpretation. Data interpretation in fact books has been accomplished for the most part by presentation of data in tables, figures, graphs, and other visual representations of data, and has generally relied on readers to generate their own conclusions. If this method has worked, it has been because most fact book readers are familiar with the nature of the data, the institution, and higher education. Marks, Endo, and Tomlinson (this volume), among others, would argue that leaving interpretation entirely to the reader is too risky and they suggest that fact book editors do some of the interpretation for the reader. Although these arguments would be countered by those who think fact books should be "neutral" or that the data should speak for themselves, there is merit in calling attention to the subtleties of the data and their implications for the institution. This is particularly true for fact books that have public relations as a primary purpose and a readership that may not be so knowledgeable about the intricacies of the institution or higher education. And if on-campus readers are as ill-informed about issues in higher education as I suggest in my closing chapter, an argument could be made for more interpretation of data rather than less. Perhaps, as I suggest there, using the fact book as a kind of textbook and including a selective bibliography to help provide a fuller context for the data would help achieve a fuller understanding of the data and the issues.

The fact book has made two other significant contributions to institutional reporting, and specifically to the interpretation of institutional data: the first is in data definitions and the second is in consistency in data reporting. Because fact books are generally public documents and because fact books report data that are often used in making institutional comparisons, there has been a movement (albeit a slow one) toward using generally accepted definitions of commonly reported fact book data. In part this could be a result of the common data definitions put forward by Integrated Postsecondary Education Data Survey (IPEDS) reporting, and in part it has come about by the growing number of institutional data exchanges. Institutional researchers are not likely to generate slightly different data sets to answer basically the same question, so acceptance of common definitions and codes has been reflected in some of the data reported in fact books, to the benefit of data interpretation across institutions and higher education generally. Tomlinson, in Chapter Six, describes why and how she includes a glossary of terms in her fact book.

In the second case, consistency of reporting, there is generally a compulsion among fact book editors to report data in the same way from one year to the next, and to note where, when, and why the data are different from those previously reported. That was not always true when the data were reported ad hoc from one year to the next, and Leischuck (1970) suggests that "pressure for consistent data" was an important reason for institutional research offices to produce fact books (p. 58). In fact, an early regional fact book on higher education had as a purpose the encouragement of "uniform reporting throughout the region" (Folger and Sugg, 1956, p. iii). Without that consistency and uniformity, data interpretation is most difficult if not impossible.

Finally, I think it can be said that the fact book reflects the best thinking and understanding of the institutional researchers that edit them. When they know something new or different, or have a new or better way of describing or explaining something, that is reflected in the next edition of the fact book.

Issue Identification. It might well be said that the first identification of institutional issues made by fact books is in their table of contents. The frequently included topics covered by fact books (see Chapter Three) include the laundry list of issues in higher education. More critically, the data presented in those sections of fact books quickly lead to a quantitative insight into the nature of the problem . . . for good or for ill. Because the fact book often represents the only public presentation of significant institutional data related to the operation of the college or university, the fact book is often the only reference faculty, students, parents, and other publics have of defining or confirming institutional problems. It is known that in some reaccreditation reviews, the fact book is used by the examiners to identify potential problems before the visitation. Clearly the presentation of data suitable for trend analysis can help institutional decision makers identify issues, and often departments, schools, colleges, and programs can identify issues particular to their programs by viewing the data for other campus units. I learned not to be surprised when fact books from other institutions were forwarded to me with questions about why our numbers didn't look as good as those of the other institutions. Current students of higher education have wondered aloud, in a course on institutional research, how institutions identified any problems before fact books were published. Pictures may say more than a thousand words, but data can generate a thousand questions. I've lost count of the number of colleagues who have "innocently" identified campus issues by either proposing the inclusion of specific data in their fact books or by actually publishing it. If one purpose of institutional research is to identify issues, the fact book is certainly a useful messenger and medium. Both Marks and Endo suggest that issue-oriented fact books need to be more widely used and developed by institutions to more directly address campus concerns, initiatives, and programs, and Tomlinson describes how and why she does it in her fact book (Chapters Two, Three, and Six). Electronic fact books, according to Daly and Viehland (Chapter Five), provide the greatest opportunity to customize the fact book to a particular topic or issue, and may represent the major reason for their development. The purpose of the issue-centered fact books would be to provide more data, detail, comparisons, interpretation, and focus for decision makers on a particular topic and related areas, clearly paving the way for meeting the next institutional research-reporting objective.

Issue Resolution. It would be interesting to know just how often a fact book is used to discover, identify, or resolve some campus question or issue. Based on the number of times in my experience that I could refer someone to the fact book for the information they were seeking, I'd say it would be a staggering number of times. In some cases the calls suggested to me that the fact book information was going to be used to settle some trivia question, but more often the question had roots in a more serious issue facing a student, faculty member, or campus administrator, and on occasion, a newspaper reporter, researcher, legislative assistant, or parent. If my experience and the similar experience of a number of other fact book editors is any indication, there certainly seems to be more evidence that fact books are being used as a source of information than evidence to the contrary: evidence resting in part on the number of inquiries to fact book editors about when the next issue will be published, and suggestions by readers for new data, editorial comments (corrections), and questions that are based on fact book data but go beyond the scope of the data presented.

Perhaps the most significant issue resolved by fact books is the one of correct data. Although it is still possible to get several different answers to the same question on any campus (and all technically correct), the fact book has become *the* source of the answer for most campuses. Fact books have probably been the major contributors to consistency and reliability in the reporting of institutional data and consequently a contributing factor in the increasing use of data in institutional management as well (West, 1983). What data or whose data to use in making institutional decisions are questions generally answered by the fact book.

As *the* source of quantitative information for a number of campus issues and activities (for example, planning, programming, assessment, evaluation) the fact book on many campuses has become a major resource in campus deliberations and directly or indirectly helps decide, if not resolve, a number of pressing campus issues. There is growing evidence, based on references to fact-book-based information in accreditation guidelines (Southern Association of Colleges and Schools, 1974), requests from governing boards and legislative bodies for fact book data, and the sharing of fact books and fact book data among and between institutions, that the fact book is the source of information for decision making by external groups and constituencies as well.

Evaluation. Because of the heavy reliance on data to document educational and institutional progress, the fact book has become one of the primary resources in producing evidence that the institution is accomplishing its mission, goals, and objectives. In fact, it is not unusual for the contents of a fact book to be organized around stated institutional objectives. It is clear that the fact book is used internally for evaluation purposes by administrators at all levels, including boards of trustees. It is also clear that the fact book is used by external evaluators, as in accreditation self studies, with legislatures, and various other governing and coordinating boards, and even in grant proposals and fundraising efforts. It is hard to imagine an evaluation exercise that wouldn't or couldn't use the fact book as an essential resource and reference when measuring institutional attainment: the fact book has clearly met this institutional research reporting objective. Yet, it must be said that evaluation is the one institutional research reporting objective that is at risk for most fact books.

There is, it seems, among institutional researchers and academic administrators a growing realization that educational and institutional program review, accountability, assessment, accreditation, or any other form of evaluation depends, or should depend, on more than numbers alone. The move away from number-driven standards by several regional accreditation groups to a more complete examination of outcomes and effectiveness may mark the most visible shift away from counting to judge the merits of an institution or program to a more systematic linking of measures with specific goals to determine accomplishment.

It is this shift in the type and use of data in the evaluation process—a shift that institutional research is currently in the process of making on most campuses—that most fact books have yet to make and which, I think, they must make if they are to keep pace with the needs of the institutions and publics they serve. The shift should not be difficult to make. As institutions shift their focus from counting to measuring, institutional data and reporting can and will reflect the shift, and the fact book will provide a perfect medium for presenting the findings. More difficult, perhaps, will be gaining institutional support for publicly reporting the information. Given the choice, however (and there may be no choice considering the success of the college rating issues of *U.S. News and World Report* and *Money* magazines), of institutions self-reporting the data and the analysis or allowing others to report the data for them, most institutions should see the merit in reporting it themselves. Better for all, in my opinion, that the fact book remain the primary source of data for institutional evaluation than the alternatives now in place.

Future of the Fact Book

It is often suggested that the reason for studying history is preparation for the future. What can be gleaned from this brief historical review of the fact book that might point to the future of the institutional fact book? Several things come to mind.

First, the fact book is an institutional research report and must continue to reflect the best of institutional research practice. What the fact book is or becomes will reflect not only on the institution but on the institutional research practitioner as well.

Second, the fact book was created and developed to fill a void in the data and information administrators and educators found necessary to do their work and, if the fact book doesn't continue to meet that need, something or somebody else will move in to do it: witness the college guides and ratings that have developed in recent years.

Third, the fact book must continue to be responsive not only to institutional needs, but to the latest and best technology for meeting those needs. As new and better ways are found to provide access to data, the fact book must respond in kind.

Fourth, in Army recruiting terminology, the fact book must be all that it can be. The fact book can and should be more than just an inanimate data repository: it can and should be actively used as a tool along with the data to achieve all those things we use data to accomplish.

If, as Leischuck (1970) suggests, "the fact book has really as many uses as staff, resources, creativeness, and ingenuity will permit" (p. 60), then I would say the historical record suggests that the creativeness and ingenuity of institutional researchers will lead to a very good fact book future.

References

Anderson, J. A., Carter, D. J., and Malizio, A. G. (eds.). *1989–90 Fact Book on Higher Education.* Washington, D.C.: American Council on Education, 1989.

Association for Institutional Research. *Forum Proceedings 1981 and Directory 1981–82*. Tallahassee, Fla.: Association for Institutional Research, 1981.

Axt, R. G. "Foreword." In *The Fact Book on Western Higher Education*. Boulder, Colo.: Western Institute Commission for Higher Education, 1960.

Bluhm, H. P. "The Place of Institutional Research in the Organizational Structure: Publications and Reports." In C. T. Stewart (ed.), *Institutional Research and Institutional Policy Formulation*. Tallahassee, Fla.: Association for Institutional Research, 1971.

Eck, J. "College and University Fact Books: A Functional Analysis." Report, Institute of Higher Education, University of Georgia, 1996.

Elliott, S. "The History of Fact Books in Higher Education." Report, Institute of Higher Education, University of Georgia, 1996.

Enarson, H. L. "Foreword." In R. G. Axt and H. T. Sprague (eds.), *College Self Study: Lectures on Institutional Research*. Boulder, Colo.: Western Interstate Commission for Higher Education, 1960.

Fincher, C., and McCord, M. *Management Concepts in Academic Administration*. Athens: Institute of Higher Education, University of Georgia, 1973.

Flint, C. C. "Institutional Research at Foothill College." *Institutional Research in the Junior College*. Occasional Report No. 3. Los Angeles: Junior College Leadership Program, School of Education, University of California, 1962.

Folger, J. K., and Sugg, R. S., Jr. (eds.) *Fact Book on Higher Education in the South*. Atlanta, Ga.: Southern Regional Education Board, 1956.

Godwin, W. L. "Foreword." In E. F. Schietinger (ed.), *Introductory Papers on Institutional Research*. Atlanta, Ga.: Southern Regional Education Board, 1968.

Gusler, T. E. "Fact Books: Paper-Based or Electronic?" In *Strategic Choice: Making Better Decisions Through Better Understanding of Institutions and Their Environments*. Proceedings of the annual conference of the North East Association for Institutional Research, Providence, R.I., Oct. 1988.

Holmes, B. D. *Managing Institutional Research at the Small College*. Fayetteville, N.C.: Fayetteville State University, 1976.

Howard, R. D., and McWhorter, M. "Fact Books: A Tool for Intra-institutional Communication." Paper presented at the Southern Conference on Institutional Research, Atlanta, Ga., Oct. 1977.

Kirks, J. L. "Workable Methods of Communicating Institutional Research Data." In P. S. Wright (ed.), *Institutional Research and Communication in Higher Education*. Tallahassee, Fla.: Association for Institutional Research, 1968.

Leischuck, G. S. "Communicating the Results of Institutional Research: The Production and Uses of the Fact Book." In P. S. Wright (ed.), *Institutional Research and Communication in Higher Education*. Tallahassee, Fla.: Association for Institutional Research, 1970.

Lins, L. J. "The Association for Institutional Research — A History." In C. H. Bagley (ed.), *Research on Academic Input*. Tallahassee, Fla.: Association for Institutional Research, 1966.

Marks, J. L. (ed.). *SREB Fact Book on Higher Education, 1994/1995*. Atlanta, Ga.: Southern Regional Education Board, 1996a.

Marks, J. L. (ed.). *SREB Fact Book on Higher Education: Georgia Highlights 1994/1995*. Atlanta, Ga.: Southern Regional Education Board, 1996b.

Montgomery, J. R. "Institutional Research—A Future Unfolding." In G. N. Drewry (ed.), *The Instructional Process and Institutional Research*. Tallahassee, Fla.: Association for Institutional Research, 1967.

Nichols, J. O., Howard, R. D., and Sharp, B. H. "The Institutional Factbook: Key to Perception of Institutional Research and Information Dissemination on the Campus." In J. Muffo and G. McLaughlin (eds.), *A Primer on Institutional Research*. Tallahassee, Fla.: Association for Institutional Research, 1987.

Roueche, J. E., and Boggs, J. R. *Junior College Institutional Research: The State of the Art*. Washington, D.C.: American Association of Junior Colleges, 1968.

Saupe, J., and Montgomery, J. R. *The Nature and Role of Institutional Research. . . Memo to a College or University*. Tallahassee, Fla.: Association for Institutional Research, 1970.

Schietinger, E. F. "Preface." In E. F. Schietinger (ed.), *Introductory Papers on Institutional Research*. Atlanta, Ga.: Southern Regional Education Board, 1968.

Smartt, S. H. (ed.), and Godwin, W. L. "Foreword." In *Fact Book on Higher Education in the South, 1979 and 1980*. Atlanta, Ga.: Southern Regional Education Board, 1980.

Smith, G. "Systematic Information Sharing in Participative University Management." *Journal of Higher Education*, 1980, *51* (5), pp. 519, 526.

Smith, G., and Strickland, W. G. "Moving Live Information to the Constituencies." *Planning for Higher Education*, 1979, *8* (1), 28–32.

Southern Association of Colleges and Schools. *Manual for Institutional Self-Study Program of the Commission on Colleges*. Atlanta, Ga.: Southern Association of Colleges and Schools, 1974.

Sprague, H. T. "Reports on Research Projects in Higher Education." In G. K. Smith (ed.), *Current Issues in Higher Education*. Washington, D.C.: Association for Higher Education, 1960.

Staskey, P. J. *Issues for the Eighties*. Tallahassee, Fla.: Association for Institutional Research, 1979.

Wechsler, H. S. "Foreword." In *The NEA 1994 Almanac of Higher Education*. Washington, D.C.: National Education Association, 1994.

West, E. D. Unpublished memo to C. R. Griffith, Office of Statistical Information and Research, American Council on Education, Washington, D.C., July 17, 1957.

West, E. D. (ed.). "Foreword." In *Fact Book on Higher Education*. Washington, D.C.: American Council on Education, 1984.

LARRY G. JONES is public service associate and associate professor in the Institute of Higher Education at the University of Georgia.

Fact books can evolve into a new generation of quintessential institutional research reports offering more of the comparative and unit- or topic-specific focus that better serves today's decision-making climate.

Toward a New Breed of Fact Book

Joseph L. Marks

A fact book is in many ways the quintessential institutional research report—a work defining the essence of the profession, a work embodying the core principles, values, and skills. The fundamental principle that underlies fact books is that documented knowledge of the college campus or multicampus system contributes to a better basis for decision making than personal memory, anecdote, and bias alone. Knowing the score is better than flying by the seat of your pants. Having indicators, even imperfect ones, is preferable to proceeding based solely on the balance of competing opinions. Although any specific fact or indicator can be criticized, and some may be discarded as fatally flawed, that should not be a rationale for avoiding a data-based approach. Better data do indeed chase out worse data in a decision-making context that is not hopelessly politicized. Using a data-based approach fundamentally changes the journey and, for colleges and universities, the journey counts. How colleges and universities conduct their business and make decisions is part of what they teach. In short, the politics of decision making is transformed and, in effect, civilized through an empirical approach to educational decision making.

Types of Fact Books and Purposes They Serve

There are two basic types of fact books: *local* and *comparative*. Local fact books describe current characteristics, trends, and, *at best,* internal comparisons for a specific institution or multicampus system. Some even deliberately avoid comparisons. Comparative fact books contain additional external or cross-unit comparisons of characteristics and trends.

Why do the two types of fact books exist? What different purposes do they serve? What different needs do they address? Fact books and planning go hand-in-hand. To make the many mundane logistical and short-term decisions and the more strategic and long-term decisions required to offer educational programs, basic data about the past, present, and projected future are always a desirable aid to the memories and impressions of decision makers. For example, to plan how many faculty members to hire or how many sections to offer, decision makers need some sort of estimates of how many students are expected. Out of the records used for decisions such as these, local fact books emerge as a handy, routinely available aid.

Fact books are a resource or reference document for on-campus or in-system users who must respond to questionnaires, develop grant proposals, prepare news releases, prepare budget documents, prepare self-study accreditation reports, conduct long-range planning, or prepare position papers for decision makers. They are a resource or reference (or even public relations) document for external audiences such as the press, prospective and new employees, potential donors, and prospective students and their families. They provide official current and trend information that, in some sense, tells the story of what the institution is about and how it has developed. Local fact books are typically published by individual colleges and universities, multicampus institutions, or state systems.

When elements of competition come into play, as in resource allocation decisions or in recruitment plans, comparisons become important. Fact books with comparative data are most often published by regional and national organizations such as the Southern Regional Education Board in its biennial *SREB Fact Book on Higher Education* or the National Center for Education Statistics' annual *Digest of Education Statistics,* or by privately developed data exchanges or cooperatives. (The State Higher Education Executive Officers' *Compendium of National Data Sources on Higher Education: A Resource Directory* contains a comprehensive listing of sources of comparative data on higher education.) Recently, state-mandated report cards and accountability reports have brought a comparative flavor to some institutional and state system reports. For example, a regional study (Bogue, Creech, and Folger, 1993) found that seven of the fifteen states that are members of the Southern Regional Education Board compact (Arkansas, Florida, Kentucky, Louisiana, South Carolina, Tennessee, and West Virginia) have accountability legislation requiring periodic reporting on a cluster of performance indicators. In five other member states (Maryland, North Carolina, Oklahoma, Texas, and Virginia) legislation requires the state higher education agencies or special task forces to develop and report on measures of higher education's effectiveness. The majority of the resulting reports incorporate cross-unit and cross-institution indicators and a few even require comparisons between states.

Are Fact Books As We Know Them Becoming Obsolete?

Local fact books are in serious need of adopting more of the comparative approach found in the regional and national fact books. With the growing emphasis on performance indicators and accountability, and with discussions of performance funding taking place in many states (to say nothing of competition over amenities for students), intercampus comparisons play an increasing role in day-to-day campus decisions, and fact books without them are rapidly becoming obsolete. Even the comparative fact books published at the regional and national levels could be more useful by spawning more customized, unit-specific reports. For example, beginning with the *SREB-State Data Exchange* report of 1988–89, the Southern Regional Education Board has periodically published state-specific summary reports along the lines suggested later in this chapter. Most recently, for the 1994/1995 edition of its biennial *SREB Fact Book on Higher Education,* the Southern Regional Education Board published a *Fact Book Highlights* book for each of the fifteen member states.

Fact books as we know them are becoming obsolete because, in large part, the context of educational decision making has changed. The locus and pace of decision making have changed. To serve new needs for long-standing users of fact books, and to serve new users (both of whom work in changed decision-making contexts) comparative information is needed. This information should be more digested and customized, be more topic- and unit-specific, and provide external as well as longitudinal comparisons.

Seeing the Future in the Current Shortcomings

Many institutional research officers (or other fact book producers) never sat or no longer sit on decision-making councils. The decision makers are still very interested in and are very much in need of the information resources of the institutional research office and fact book. Increasingly, fact book users do not have the time, inclination, or skills for transforming, analyzing, and formatting the information into usable forms. Some upper-echelon users have long used fact books as a kind of catalog from which they could order customized, unit-specific reports.

This fact about the context for fact books has led some to suggest that institutional research offices evolve from centralized data service centers into training centers for a more distributed approach to data collection, analysis, interpretation, and presentation. Having a fact book in hand on such a training mission would be useful. Besides this evolution, institutional research offices can themselves do more of the comparative, customized work that better fits today's campus and system-level decision-making context. Such customized work can either be produced separately in the form of fact book spin-offs or, possibly, be built into fact books themselves.

Database development, maintenance, and availability are as important, if not more important, now than they ever were. Producing a fact book from this database provides a standard statistical reference book for the campus or system. A purpose mentioned less frequently is how working through the data to produce a polished report exposes previously undetected or unresolved problems in the data. The extra effort expended polishing the data into a major publication may reduce the time and office resources available to provide a more useful service that creates an even better opportunity to expose the data to the corrective view of outside audiences. Putting the data before audiences in a more comparative, customized form is more attention-getting and brings out a level of problems rarely exposed. Reporting units that have verified suspect submissions repeatedly can be led to a more effective reexamination when the data appear in a comparative context that is available to significant, knowledgeable peers and colleagues.

The data in a fact book clearly needs to remain widely available, possibly through on-line data services such as the one the Southern Regional Education Board has operated since 1991, or through the growing number of World Wide Web sites. In this era of rapidly changing technologies for information sharing, it may be that scarce institutional research office resources could be better spent elsewhere than in producing a traditional fact book. For example, in place of the typical tables currently found in fact books, it would be more useful to campus administrators, faculty members, and external audiences to have available a set of customized, topic-specific (for example, enrollment, faculty salaries, degrees conferred), and unit-specific (one for each college or department) reports where longitudinal, cross campus, and external comparisons are presented. Such reports would, I believe, be more attention-getting and would be more widely read. This increased exposure could uncover more errors. More people would be led to examine their standings and think about their units in a broader context. A greater number of interesting story gems could be unearthed from the data mine. The radioactivity of a fact book spin-off can last longer than that of the source book itself. And yes, that implies that customized, topic- and unit-specific reports will be hotter to handle.

Model for a New Generation of Fact Books

Consider the following fictitious local fact book enrollment table (Table 2.1) with an added statewide (comparative) dimension:

Over the past ten years, enrollment at Old Main University grew much faster than the statewide average. Among colleges, the College of Education enrollment grew the fastest, led by graduate-level increases. Compared to statewide trends over the same time, enrollment in the College of Education at Old Main University grew twice as fast as the statewide average. Enrollment in the College of Business also grew at a rate greater than the statewide average, but only marginally so. The slowest rate of enrollment growth at Old Main University was in the College of Arts and Sciences, in contrast to the statewide pattern, where Arts and Sciences enrollment grew the fastest. Both statewide and at Old Main University, graduate enrollment in the Arts and Sciences and Education grew faster than undergraduate enrollment and, in the colleges of Business, undergraduate enrollment grew the fastest.

Fact books as we know them (local or comparative) contain hundreds of informative tables. Local fact books most often contain little other than tables

Table 2.1. Head Count Enrollment by College and Level

	1984–85	1994–95	Percentage Increase
Mother Earth Statewide Total	98,150	103,923	5.9
Arts and Sciences	31,500	33,810	7.3
Undergraduate	20,932	22,397	7.0
Graduate	10,568	11,413	8.0
Business	36,121	37,519	3.9
Undergraduate	28,532	29,702	4.1
Graduate	11,543	12,374	7.2
Education	30,529	32,594	6.8
Undergraduate	18,986	20,220	6.5
Graduate	11,543	12,374	7.2
Old Main University Total	6,199	6,671	7.6
Arts and Sciences	1,437	1,470	2.3
Undergraduate	1,112	1,135	2.1
Graduate	325	335	3.2
Business	2,389	2,502	4.7
Undergraduate	1,543	1,623	5.2
Graduate	846	879	4.0
Education	2,373	2,699	13.7
Undergraduate	1,327	1,490	12.3
Graduate	1,046	1,209	15.6

and descriptive information about campus history, services, and offerings. Few describe findings from the data. Those that do usually contain only very brief highlights for each chapter. In my review of fact books I found that only one out of every five institutional or system fact books contained *any* description of findings. Regional or national fact books more often contain extended highlights describing key findings but rarely explore questions arising from the findings.

Although adding descriptions and exploring questions arising from the findings would be desirable, a much more attention-getting approach is to prepare a set of reports (enrollment, for example) illustrated like a slide show, one for each college, school, division, department, or program. A sketch of what part of such a report for a College of Arts and Sciences might look like follows (see Figure 2.1).

Advantages of the New Approach. The illustrated approach has advantages. It helps readers visualize relationships and focus on the position of the home unit. It also makes questions jump out at the reader more, questions such as why certain differences exist. For example, the sample calls attention to an asymmetry between the Old Main University and the statewide-by-college enrollment patterns. Why was Arts and Sciences enrollment growth lowest among colleges at Old Main but highest among colleges statewide? Why was the College of Education enrollment growth highest at Old Main but much lower statewide? It is helpful to have these questions raised so that promising

Figure 2.1. Arts and Sciences Enrollment, 1984–85 to 1994–95

Over the past 10 years, the number of students enrolled at Old Main University has increased faster (7.6 percent) than the state-wide average of 5.9 percent. The number of Arts and Sciences students at Old Main increased less than the number enrolled in the colleges of Business and Education. Statewide, among the three colleges, Arts and Sciences enrollment grew fastest.

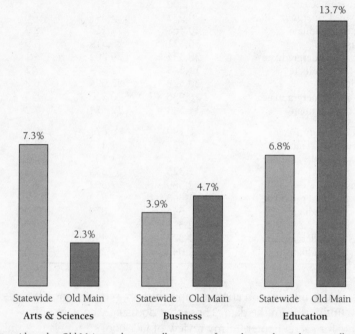

Both statewide and at Old Main, graduate enrollment grew faster than undergraduate enrollment in the colleges of Arts and Sciences and Education. In colleges of Business, undergraduate enrollment grew faster.

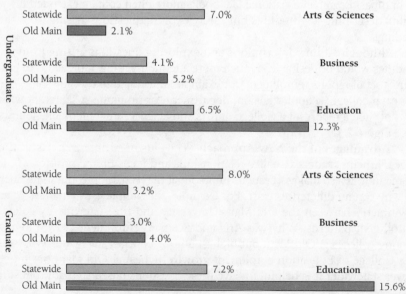

further research is identified and the campus or systemwide community becomes more aware of key differences and trends.

Clearly, fact books as we know them contain useful information and a solid foundation for reports about a campus or multicampus system. They can evolve into a new generation of quintessential institutional research reports, if more customized, topic- or unit-specific reports are spawned. Institutional researchers can provide better service and be a more important and valued part of their professional scene, if they evolve from being keepers of the data to being helpers in their communities' search for what the numbers mean.

One way to give the numbers more meaning is through comparative, topic- or unit-specific reports. This is a higher profile approach and entails some risk. It will make waves where there may have been few. Moving from collecting and presenting data to exhibiting and interpreting it can create movement in a desirable direction. Conflicts and differences of opinion may develop that can lead to an increased understanding of colleges and universities, to better data, better means of exhibiting them, and to better interpretations of what, when, where, how, and why things are the way they are. It may also suggest approaches to educational improvement.

For example, the sample customized report could help leaders at Old Main University to evaluate whether the different directions of their enrollment trends from the statewide pattern are a cause for concern. Were students moving from Arts and Sciences to Education because of new teacher certification requirements in effect in the Old Main service area? Did changes in statewide admissions requirements move Arts and Sciences students to a larger nearby university? Was the low growth in Arts and Sciences due to a court-ordered transfer of graduate programs? Was a change in the way enrollment records are kept by including off-campus students doing internships a big factor? Did the new younger leadership and the retirement in the College of Education of half of the old guard play a role?

Conclusion

Colleges and universities today operate with resource constraints, growing public skepticism, and rapid economic and social changes. Significant enrollment growth and changing demographic characteristics of students are projected over the next two decades. As colleges and universities face these challenges, institutional research offices have an important opportunity to reshape and improve their services. The fact book spin-off adopting the illustrated, comparative approach, is a promising vision of the institutional research of tomorrow and of the fact books of tomorrow.

References

Bogue, G., Creech, J., and Folger, J. *Assessing Quality and Effectiveness in Higher Education: Work in Progress.* Atlanta, Ga.: Southern Regional Education Board, 1993.

Marks, J. L. *SREB Fact Book on Higher Education 1994/1995*. Atlanta, Ga.: Southern Regional Education Board, 1994.

Russell, A., and Rodriguez, E. *A Compendium of National Data Sources on Higher Education: A Resource Directory*. Denver, Colo.: State Higher Education Executive Officers, 1993.

Snyder, T. D., and Hoffman, C. M. *Digest of Education Statistics 1995*. Washington, D.C.: National Center for Education Statistics, 1995.

JOSEPH L. MARKS is associate director for data services at the Southern Regional Education Board, Atlanta, Georgia.

Fact books can differ in the information they contain and the manner in which it is presented, but there are useful strategies for developing the contents of a general purpose fact book for individual colleges and universities.

Developing the Contents of Institutional Fact Books

Jean J. Endo

Institutional researchers and others most often develop fact books for individual colleges and universities. However, they can create fact books for multi-institution systems or state, regional, or national-level groupings of schools and, at the other end of the spectrum, for institutional units such as academic departments. This chapter is a brief introduction to strategies for developing the contents of a fact book for individual colleges and universities.

Existing institutional fact books vary in the topics they cover, the breadth and depth of the information they include, and the manner in which information is presented. One primary reason for this is that fact books have been designed for different purposes and to meet the needs and preferences of different audiences. The significance of purposes and audience needs and preferences underlies many of the ideas in this chapter. Whereas the crucial nature of these factors is obvious, specific efforts must be made to ensure that they receive the attention necessary to produce a successful fact book.

Initial Considerations

There are four initial considerations that have an important bearing on fact book development. First, there must be agreement about the main purposes of a fact book because its contents must be directly related to these objectives. In general, institutions develop one or more fact books for several reasons. Fact books provide various internal and external audiences (for example, campus administrators, faculty, staff, governing boards, legislators, state agencies, prospective or current students and their parents, news media, potential donors, and other segments of the public) with basic information that: (1) gives them an overall picture of the institution, or (2) allows them to generally assess aspects of the institution, or (3) provides background for material such as management reports, accreditation self-studies, news releases, and other public-relations-oriented communication, and so forth. Fact books also support planning at the institution, school, college, or department levels. They can provide the individuals involved (for example, senior-level executives, deans, or department chairs) with a common set of accurate and consistent background information, and they help identify priorities, issues, and problems, thereby contributing to the planning agenda. In addition, fact books can be helpful in making specific short-term administrative decisions as well as longer-range decisions. (Of course, institutions use additional sources of information for decision-support and to do planning, including topical or special institutional research reports and data tables.)

A second initial consideration has to do with the circumstances under which a fact book is produced. When time or resources are limited (or if the fact book is a preliminary, first-time effort), institutions often produce a quick version of a fact book that addresses only the most frequently asked questions or most important issues and includes information that is readily available or easily compiled (for example, information on the numbers and characteristics of students and faculty, and program enrollments). When more time or resources are available, institutions can produce a longer and more detailed version of a fact book that has a broader scope and necessitates a more systematic and time-consuming process of information-gathering and analysis. The discussion in this chapter will be most relevant for the longer version of a fact book, although the ideas need to be considered in some abbreviated fashion for shorter versions as well.

A third initial consideration involves the differences between an issues-oriented fact book and a general purpose fact book. An issues-oriented fact book focuses on a particular topic (for example, student enrollments, faculty characteristics, or financial aid) or institutional unit(s) and provides extensive detail designed to answer specific questions. For instance, an ethnic minority faculty retention fact book might be geared to answering the following questions:

What is the pool of potential ethnic minority faculty in various disciplines nationwide?
How interested are ethnic minority candidates in applying for tenure-track positions at college X?
How successful are ethnic minority candidates in securing tenure-track positions at college X?
How successful are nontenured ethnic minority faculty in securing tenure at college X?
Once tenured, how long do ethnic minority faculty stay at college X?

This type of fact book might include discipline-specific historical data on the numbers of doctoral degrees awarded to ethnic minorities in the United States;

the numbers of ethnic minority candidates who applied for tenure-track positions at college X, who were hired, and who achieved tenure; comparisons of such numbers with those of comparable institutions; and other data, including qualitative information related to ethnic minority faculty retention. In contrast, a general purpose fact book would address much more than a particular topic. This chapter will discuss the development of a general purpose fact book, though the ideas in a modified form also have applicability for an issues-oriented fact book.

Finally, several disciplines (for example, communications, business management and information systems, psychology, and English) offer ideas on organizing and presenting information. Considering such ideas can improve the quality of a fact book. See, for example, Browne and Keeley (1994), Sapp (1994), Hackman (1983), Ewell (1989), and Adler and van Doren (1972).

Getting Started

An excellent way to begin developing the contents of a fact book is to determine a set of primary and secondary questions that it attempts to answer. Keeping in mind the purposes of the fact book, there are a number of specific ways to come up with key questions, for instance by using brainstorming techniques, doing analyses of existing fact books (including any previously produced at the institution), examining the institution's mission statement or any strategic planning objectives that have been developed (for example, increasing student retention), and identifying benchmarks of high-priority operations to monitor institutional health, including indicators of successful institutional performance. These efforts should involve representatives of the audience for which the fact book is being developed, and the offices from which information must be gathered to ensure their cooperation.

As previously mentioned, examining existing fact books is one way of determining primary and secondary questions. Table 3.1 lists the contents of general purpose fact books I recently reviewed that were produced at over thirty four-year private and public colleges and universities throughout the United States. The table shows the range of items found in these fact books and should not be seen as a list of necessary items. The items most common to these fact books dealt with student enrollment and demographic characteristics, numbers and characteristics of faculty, degrees awarded, the academic potential of new students, tuition and fees, and current funds revenues.

For many fact book purposes, an institution's mission statement or strategic planning objectives are invaluable for determining primary and secondary questions. When thinking about these sources, consider collecting or producing more detailed or fully analyzed information even if only aggregate-level information is needed for the fact book. For example, it may be sufficient to have a fact book table that shows the numbers of ethnic minority and nonminority faculty by academic unit. When gathering this information, it may be useful to first get data on the numbers of faculty by specific ethnic minority group. This level of detail may be unnecessary for the fact book, but it would

Table 3.1. Range of Items in a Sample of Institution-Wide General Purpose Factbooks

General Information

> Role and mission statement
> Strategic planning goals
> Academic calendar
> History of the institution/timeline of major events
> Members of the governing board
> Organization charts
> Accreditations
> Peer institutions

Information on Students

> Numbers of new applicants, admits and enrollees
> > Freshman students
> > Transfer students
> > Graduate students

> Academic potential of new students
> > College entrance test scores (ACT, SAT)
> > High school percentile ranks
> > High school grade point averages
> > College grade point averages
> > Other test scores (for example, GRE and LSAT)

> Other information on new students
> > Feeder high schools for freshmen
> > Competing institutions for new freshmen
> > Previous institutions of new transfer students and graduate students
> > Demographic characteristics of new freshmen, transfer students and graduate students

> Numbers of readmitted students

> Headcount enrollments
> > Fall term
> > Term by term
> > Summer session(s)
> > By level (for example, undergraduate/graduate)

> Full-time equivalent (FTE) enrollments
> > Academic year
> > Fall term
> > Term by term
> > Summer session(s)
> > By level

> Headcount/FTE ratios

> Demographic characteristics
> > Gender, age, race/ethnicity
> > International student status
> > Marital status
> > Residency status

Table 3.1. (continued)

Retention/attrition rates of new freshmen cohorts
Graduation rates of new freshmen cohorts

Salaries of graduate assistants and associates
Employment status and salaries of recent graduates
  By degree type and/or discipline

Credit hour loads
  Term by term
  By full-time/part-time status

Numbers of students by discipline/major
  By gender, race/ethnicity
  By international student status

Grades awarded and/or grade point averages
  By academic unit/discipline
  By level

Numbers of students receiving academic honors
Numbers of students on academic suspension

Home area of new freshmen or all students
Local area of residence of all students
International student enrollment by country

Information on Degrees

Numbers and types of degrees awarded
  By gender and race/ethnicity
  By other demographic characteristics
  By term or fiscal year
  By academic unit/discipline

Distinguished recipients of honorary degrees

Information on Costs and Financial Aid

Typical costs of attending the institution
  Tuition and mandatory fees
  Room and board
  Other costs (for example, books and travel)

Financial aid sources and types
Numbers of students receiving financial aid
  By gender, age, and race/ethnicity
  By level
  By residency status
  By other demographic characteristics

Information on Faculty

Numbers of new faculty and all faculty
  By academic unit/discipline
  By rank
  By tenure and tenure-track status
  By full- and part-time institutional status

Table 3.1. *(continued)*

Other characteristics of new faculty and all faculty
  Demographic characteristics
  Highest degrees earned
  Institutions awarding highest degrees to faculty
  Academic honors/distinctions
  Local area of residence

Names of department chairs, other administrators
Names of faculty holding endowed chairs

Faculty salaries by rank

Faculty workload by academic unit/discipline
  FTE student/faculty ratios
  Student credit hours per faculty FTE
  Average class sizes

Information on Staff

Numbers by administrative unit and job type
Demographic characteristics
Local area of residence

Information on Continuing Education Programs

Courses/Activities
Enrollments in credit and noncredit courses

Institutional Expenditures and Resources

Current funds revenues and expenditures
Contracts and grants, sponsored programs
Patents and licenses
Market value of endowments
Private gift support
Alumni contributions

Research centers, laboratories, and other research facilities
Information technology facilities and services
Library holdings and other resources

New buildings and building renovations
  Net assignable square feet
  Total gross square feet by functional area
  Academic and research space allocations
Classroom utilization data
Inventory of land
  Campus size
  Buildings (age, gross area, useable area)
  Streets and parking spaces
  Student and faculty housing
Property values

Economic impact of the institution

Special Features
Bullet summaries of important trends
Summary of main facts

Table 3.1. (*continued*)

Summary of campus services and organizations
List of fraternities and sororities
Special student activities
Special academic programs
Special athletic accomplishments

External comparisons of data on students and faculty
  (for example, with comparable institutions or those in the same region

Campus map
Definition of terms and data
Questionnaire for users to provide feedback
Index

be available for follow-up informational requests, supplemental fact book pages or sections, issues-oriented fact books, customized reports for specific users, and later data needs for strategic planning purposes.

Benchmarks of high-priority operations might include items like dropout rates, test scores of new students, student-to-faculty ratios, and alumni contributions. For possible benchmarks, see the articles by Sapp (1994) and Borden and Banta (1994) on indicators of successful institutional performance. Another good way of identifying benchmarks is to look at information that is used to make comparisons between institutions, such as that reported by data-exchange consortia like the Association of American Universities, the Higher Education Data-Sharing Consortium (Franklin and Marshall College), and College Information Systems (Auburn University). For a discussion of inter-institutional comparisons, see Brinkman (1987). Also, regional organizations, including the Western Interstate Commission on Higher Education and the Southern Regional Education Board, and national organizations, including the National Center for Education Statistics, publish reports with comparative information.

Following are some examples of general primary (P) and secondary (S) questions:

(P) How large is college X?
(S) How many students are enrolled?
(S) How many faculty and staff are employed?
(S) How many acres of land comprise the total campus?
(P) How selective is college X?
(S) What are the mean high school grade point averages of new fall term freshmen?
(S) What are the mean college entrance test scores of new fall term freshmen?
(S) How many prospective new freshmen apply for the fall term? Of these, how many are accepted, and how many actually enroll?
(S) What are the graduation rates for cohorts of new fall term freshmen?
(S) What are the academic qualifications of new transfer students and new graduate students?

(P) How is college X organized?

(S) What is the governing structure?

(S) What is the mission statement?

(S) What do its organization charts look like?

(P) What are the characteristics of the students enrolled at college X?

(S) What are the percentages of women and men?

(S) What are the percentages of ethnic minority students?

(S) What is the percentage of international students?

(S) What is the percentage of out-of-state students?

(S) From what geographic areas do students come?

(S) What are the percentages of undergraduates and graduate students?

(S) What is the percentage of part-time students?

(P) What happens to the graduates of college X?

(S) How successful are undergraduate degree recipients in obtaining admission to graduate and professional schools?

(S) What types of jobs do undergraduate and graduate and professional degree recipients obtain?

(P) How expensive is college X?

(S) What are the resident and nonresident tuition and fees for undergraduates and graduate students?

(S) What is the cost of room and board?

(S) What is the typical cost of books and supplies?

(P) What are the characteristics of the faculty at college X?

(S) What are the percentages of women and men?

(S) What are the percentages of ethnic minority faculty?

(S) What is the percentage of part-time faculty?

(S) What percentage of the faculty have earned doctorates?

(S) What major honors and awards have faculty members received?

(S) What is the average salary by rank?

(P) What resources are available at college X?

(S) How many books are in the library?

(S) What kinds of computer facilities, research centers, laboratories, and other resources are available for teaching and research?

Important Issues

It may seem obvious that a fact book should contain sufficient information on all its major topics. However, this is not always the case. Sometimes, for instance, fact books contain a good deal of information on students but relatively little on other aspects of an institution. Also, fact books sometimes include relatively large amounts of the types of information that are easy to obtain (for example, on student demographic and enrollment characteristics) and less of other types that are more difficult to gather (for example, on student achievement or other educational outcomes). This can create misperceptions if fact book users associate the amount of information with the importance of a topic.

In a general purpose fact book, try not to include an excessive amount of detail given the fact book's purpose and the needs and preferences of the audience for which it is being developed. For example, if a fact book is designed to provide a variety of on-campus and external audiences with basic information that gives them an overall sense of the institution, data on overall graduation rates may be sufficient rather than graduation rates by academic unit, gender, and race or ethnicity. The latter might be more appropriate for a fact book designed to support planning on an institution-wide basis. However, it may be useful to anticipate the next level of questions that a fact book user might have. If it seems appropriate to have available more detailed information, this could go in an appendix or even a separate document.

Information in a fact book must be accurate. If necessary, recheck information on certain topics with several sources. Only use research data from studies that are well-designed and executed and that use the appropriate methodology (Jones, 1989). Present research data in simple and straightforward terms, for instance, by using percentages, means, or bivariate crosstabular tables. One way to handle research findings based on complex analyses is to briefly describe them in a narrative fashion.

The general manner in which information is presented in a fact book is very important. Obtain feedback about this from representatives of the audience for which the fact book is being developed. For example, the latter might prefer large or small proportions of graphs, tables, charts, diagrams, and written materials such as interpretations and summaries. Some individuals might prefer smaller pages or even a pocket-sized format (which is especially suitable for widely distributed, public-relations-oriented fact books). Fact book information can be presented in a bound document or in a loose-leaf binder that easily accommodates changes and updates. Some individuals might prefer to access information electronically and to be able to customize the type, detail level, and display of data (see the chapter by Daly and Viehland in this volume on electronic fact books). Consult other institutions' fact books to get ideas. If an institution previously has produced fact books, these provide a basis for presenting information.

Organize the information in a fact book so that it appears in a concise and logical manner. For instance, group information into sets or clusters based on importance, generality or specificity, interest to readers, similarities or differences, time period, or other criteria. Try to place closely related items on the same page or adjacent pages so that their relationships will be most apparent. Try carefully compressing some secondary information (for example, by using small print fonts) so readers can focus on the more important items.

Sometimes, it may be useful for a single fact book page to contain the most important information for understanding a particular topic. As an example, information on headcount enrollment by residency status might be presented with a data table showing enrollment by residency status for the past five years, a graph of the latter directly above the table, one or two smaller data tables containing more detailed information for the most recent year (such as headcount enrollment by residency status by undergraduate and graduate levels), and brief written interpretations of the most significant data trends and differences using a bullet-summary format.

Consider memory-facilitating techniques based on principles from cognitive theory and information processing, for instance, using seven or fewer categories in tables. In graphical displays, the patterns should clearly distinguish the different items being graphed. If possible, use the same patterns for the same items throughout the fact book, and give each graph a legend that identifies the patterns used. Give graphs, tables, diagrams, and maps short, self-explanatory titles, and be consistent in the terminology used in titles, headings and subheadings, labels, footnotes, and so forth.

Other elements of a fact book's physical appearance can vary and should depend on the needs and preferences of the audience for which the fact book is being developed. Visual appeal is likely to be more important in public-relations-oriented fact books for external audiences. On the other hand, an emphasis on simplicity and consistency may appeal to other audiences as a way of better understanding complex issues. See the chapter by Thompson in this volume for a discussion of fact book layout and design. Tufte (1983) also is a good reference that deals with the display of quantitative data.

Use footnotes to define terms and assumptions, provide data definitions, explain discrepancies (for example, between specific types of data presented for different years), identify information sources, or answer obvious questions that might arise (for example, differences between the way data are being presented now and the way they were presented in previous fact books or standard reports produced at the institution). Use appendices as an alternative to footnotes when more detail is required (for example, a definition of the areas of specialization in major fields of study, or the academic units in various schools or colleges, or a listing of additional sources of data on a particular topic).

Additional Considerations

As the development of a fact book is moving along, a number of other things might require attention. Often, fact book development must take place within a specific time frame that corresponds to its purpose, for instance, before an institution's budget and planning cycle. Occasionally, the most recent needed information is not available during this time frame. Compromises then must be made. In the situation just cited, it may be best to use earlier enrollment data from the beginning of a term rather than waiting until the end of the term, and to make adjustments based on previous enrollment differences between beginning-of-term and end-of-term census dates.

If a fact book is to contain data used to illustrate historical trends, define these data in the same manner for each academic or fiscal year, term, or other time period. Note discrepancies that arise, perhaps in footnotes. One example might be the numbers of faculty by academic unit for five or ten academic years where some individuals have administrative appointments, sabbaticals, or leaves outside their unit in certain years that affect the numbers being presented.

A fact book may contain information considered by some to be sensitive or possibly to have undesirable consequences if taken out of context or misinterpreted. An example might be low graduation rates for freshman cohorts after four years. One way of dealing with this is to provide additional information, in this case, graduation rates after five or six years along with an explanation of why rates might be low after four years (for example, many students change their majors, or they work and are unable to take full course loads). Obtain ideas on presenting sensitive information from campus administrators and representatives of the audience for which the fact book is being developed.

If a fact book is to include written interpretations or summaries of data, carefully prepare these and make every attempt to avoid biases. For instance, comparisons of data on white and ethnic minority students should reflect (to the extent possible) what actually is happening rather than emphasizing a particular point of view. Sometimes, biases might be avoided simply by presenting data without offering interpretations or summaries.

If data are to be aggregated for presentation in a fact book, also do this in a careful manner to avoid biases. For example, when there are significant differences in graduation rates between (or within) ethnic minority groups, it may be preferable to report these separately for each group (or subgroup) rather than for all groups combined. Likewise, it may be preferable to report various data on ethnic minority faculty separately for each group (and by rank). In some cases, it may be satisfactory to place such disaggregated data in the fact book's appendices or to cite other sources for this information in a footnote.

If data comparisons are to be made with other institutions, use colleges or universities that are comparable on the relevant dimensions. Examples of such dimensions include type (Carnegie classification), size, public or private basis of funding, admissions selectivity, and location. In most cases, campus administrators already will have determined one or more sets of comparable institutions for internal planning and decision making purposes.

Always report information in an ethical manner. Do not knowingly include inaccurate or misleading information (for example, "cooked" data on standardized test scores).

Always allow ample time to proofread the final draft of a fact book before it is produced and distributed. Proofreaders should look for informational, spelling, grammatical, and typographical errors and check the fact book's overall organization, pagination, consistent use of terminology, and writing style in textual materials.

The purposes and anticipated specific uses of a fact book should determine the manner and extent of its distribution. See the chapter in this volume by Tomlinson on strategies for using a fact book.

In order to improve future editions, evaluate a fact book for its usefulness, accuracy, and presentation of information; and assess needed changes to incorporate new issues, sources or types of information, and perspectives. One way of doing this is to include an evaluation sheet with the fact book for users to send back. Or, try other techniques with known users, such as a telephone survey or focus group sessions.

Once produced, fact books can be updated or supplemented for various reasons by adding pages or sections, through topic-specific fact books, or by providing data through electronic means.

Conclusion

This chapter has discussed the development of the contents of a general purpose fact book for individual colleges and universities. The ideas presented here are possible approaches to the process of fact book development since there are no standard, step-by-step formulas. At many institutions, the development of fact books is or will be an ongoing process as successive editions or entirely different versions are created. Over time, these efforts will yield new ideas and caveats.

Future strategies for developing fact books will need to keep pace with changes in the informational needs and preferences of various audiences, changes in information technology, and changes in institutional research and the environments in which it operates (see Terenzini, 1995). These changes will have numerous consequences, including an increasing demand for user-tailored information, a wider availability of information generally, and a greater proliferation and dispersion of institutional research functions across campus units. The latter consequences, in turn, may lead to greater emphases on summarizing and analyzing information, organizing the flow of available information to show its proper contexts and relationships, and providing standard data definitions and rules. Fact books will need to be sensitive to such trends.

References

Adler, M., and van Doren, C. *How to Read a Book.* New York: Simon & Schuster, 1972.

Borden, V., and Banta, T. (eds.). *Using Performance Indicators to Guide Strategic Decision Making.* New Directions for Institutional Research, no. 82. San Francisco: Jossey-Bass, 1994.

Brinkman, P. (ed.). *Conducting Interinstitutional Comparisons.* New Directions for Institutional Research, no. 53. San Francisco: Jossey-Bass, 1987.

Browne, M. N., and Keeley, S. *Asking the Right Questions: A Guide to Critical Thinking.* (4th ed.) Englewood Cliffs, N.J.: Prentice Hall, 1994.

Ewell, P. (ed.). *Enhancing Information Use in Decision Making.* New Directions for Institutional Research, no. 64. San Francisco: Jossey-Bass, 1989.

Hackman, J. "Seven Maxims for Institutional Researchers: Applying Cognitive Theory and Research." *Research in Higher Education,* 1983, *18* (2), 195–268.

Jones, L. "The Institutional Research Report Revisited." In P. Ewell (ed.), *Enhancing Information Use in Decision Making.* New Directions for Institutional Research, no. 64. San Francisco: Jossey-Bass, 1989.

Sapp, M. "Setting Up a Key Success Index Report: A How-To Manual." *Association for Institutional Research Professional File,* Winter 1994, no. 51.

Terenzini, P. "Evolution and Revolution in Institutional Research." Keynote address to the annual forum of the Association for Institutional Research, Boston, May 29, 1995. (For a summary, see *Air Currents,* 1995, *33* (3–4), 7.)

Tufte, E. *The Visual Display of Quantitative Information.* Cheshire, Conn.: Graphics Press, 1983.

JEAN J. ENDO is coordinator of student planning information services in the School of Education at the University of Colorado-Denver.

This chapter offers advice on making a fact book not only more readable and appealing, but also more user-friendly.

Producing an Institutional Fact Book: Layout and Design for a User-Friendly Product

James A. Thompson

The principles of layout design and typography apply as readily to fact books as to any other publication. However, the demands placed on readers perusing a potentially tedious fact book are considerably more rigorous than the usual demands of concentration and attention to detail. Failure to produce an attractive, balanced, and judicious layout makes unfair and unrealistic demands on the users of any fact book. This chapter offers advice on making a fact book not only more readable and appealing, but also more user-friendly. Although the assumption is made that such fact books will be produced with the aid of a personal computer, the concepts presented will generally apply to the production of any printed fact book.

Hardware or Software Configuration

In the academic world of electronic desktop publishing (DTP), it is probably inconsequential as to which hardware configuration is used, whether it be the IBM platform, Macintosh, or whatever, as long as screen results are seen in Macintosh-like *what you see is what you get* (WYSIWYG) fashion, now brought about by the advent of *Windows* in most IBM compatibles. Personal preference and interoffice compatibility are probably the major factors in use or purchasing considerations. Personal preference is usually driven by software familiarity, and interoffice compatibility eases file transfer and clip art exchange from within the workplace—regardless if one is mouse or keyboard oriented.

Failure to have the latest state-of-the-art equipment does not, in itself, condemn DTP efforts to mediocrity. Central Alabama Community College (CACC) has produced fact books for years on outdated hardware, considering the fast-paced life span of computer technology. Yet in terms of production and familiarity, as well as minimal disk space requirements and internal memory, the configuration suits the minimal needs of the team members and enables a quality product to be efficiently produced. CACC uses the Apple Macintosh IIsi computer with a color Radius pivot screen, a 340 MB external hard drive, and 16 MB of internal memory. For graphics scanning, a conventional flatbed Apple scanner is used (software includes Apple's own *Apple Scan* as well as *Ofoto* for scanning of graphics—for scanning text [OCR], *Omnipage 2.0*). The college's research office prints to a simple Apple LaserWriter IInt, then usually duplicates and binds such jobs in-house. Due to budget considerations, as well as a desire to keep production as simple as possible, the research office continues to publish its fact book without the benefit of color laser print technology or color separations.

Whichever the system, good DTP software is critical. Some find Aldus's *PageMaker* program the program of choice in either the Mac or IBM platforms; others prefer *Quark* or *Ventura*. The research office at CACC uses *PageMaker* 4.2 (Macintosh version) for its DTP needs, *MacWrite II* for word processing and extensive editing, *DeltaGraph Professional* for statistical charts and graphs, *SuperPaint 2.0* for graphics, and *MacLink 2.0* for conversion of documents from IBM to Macintosh format.

Design Considerations

There are various components to consider in order to achieve an appealing fact book design.

   Balance. Good design in a fact book or any other DTP chore is achieved through a process of repeated refinements; that is, first get the content down, then keep working until it is pleasing to the eye. A key design concept here is balance.

In its simplest sense, some degree of balance should be attained between the amount of text (titles, subtitles, captions, articles, outlines, table text, histories, summaries, and the like) and visuals or graphic elements (clip art, illustrations, maps, graphs, charts, borders around tables, photographs, and so on) within the fact book. Planners and designers of an institution's fact book must determine what that balance is exactly according to user needs. As it is being planned and assimilated, planners should aim for some degree of variety in the types of information to be gathered and in the format by which that information is presented. Just as data can often be effectively displayed in either a bar graph or pie chart, the information within a fact book can be presented in any number of ways: graphically, textually, or in combination. In making assignments for fact book material or in allotting page space for the data, keep in mind the need for variety in visual presentation and try to maintain a predetermined balance between graphic and textual elements. For example, a nine-to-one ratio of visuals to text elements was attained in the most recent edition of CACC's *1993–94 Fact Book* (approximately 121 graphs, 60 tables, over 20 graphic elements such as maps or diagrams, but only 16 articles or solitary textual elements). Balancing one's fact book material with an eye for visual variety can mean the difference in appearance between, say, a text-filled page from one's local newspaper and the creatively balanced design from *USA Today*.

Of course, visual variety is not the only balance criterion. One should always first consider which particular medium (textual or graphic) is deemed more effective for optimum visual presentation of the data involved. In a fact book, aim to present the information in a compact and readily digestible format so that even the most casual peruser will gain something from flipping through its pages. The generous use of carefully tailored visuals and efficient summary-type text blocks enhances the visual effectiveness of the fact book.

Another consideration is a general level of visual balance to be maintained among the individual items on a page or page spread, whether those items are text, graphic elements, or a mixture of both. For example, a medium-sized graphic in the lower right corner of a page may need two or more smaller items (either text blocks or graphics) in the opposing corner to give the page a balanced look. One might experiment by placing the accompanying text blocks at various points on the page—perhaps varying their length, width, or even font size—until the desired look is achieved. And it is certainly appropriate to use both portrait (vertical) and landscape (horizontal) orientations in the same fact book. In fact, this would help achieve visual variety. However, because it is awkward for readers to continually shift their book this way and that, designers should attempt to keep such pages together on the same spread, or at least on consecutive pages when possible, and to choose such pages' orientation appropriately.

On the other hand, too much balance can be boring to the eyes, especially if each page of the fact book maintains the same number of columns and the same placement of graphic and textual elements throughout. Avoid visual stagnation by alternating column widths, the number of columns, and placement of graphic elements together with an appropriate extent of white space throughout the publication. It is desirable to maintain visual balance AND a degree of irregularity and creativity so that the publication has a uniform look throughout but is not dull or monotonous.

White Space. White space was previously mentioned as a variable in controlling balance. The readability of a fact book is influenced by the extent of white space used: the amount of space between text lines (leading), between letters (kerning), or the general amount of space allowed for the margins and around visuals such as graphs, diagrams, and pictures. A software manual is a good resource for information on leading and kerning. The Aldus manual that accompanied *PageMaker 4.2* was particularly helpful to me in this respect. Regarding borders, one should just understand that white space is used to emphasize textual and graphic elements by isolating them from their environment. Too little white space in the margins makes the pages appear as one gray mass, intimidating the reader on a subconscious level. The material overwhelms the reader, making the text more difficult to read and appearing (in a visual sense) unexciting and monotonous. Remember, too, that readers of fact books often scribble in the margins, so ample white space is practical as well as appealing to the eye. Try to maintain at least three-quarters of an inch for all margins, deviating only when necessary to accommodate some protruding graphic element or for the sake of balance. Leaving sufficient space between columns and between placed elements is also a consideration.

Associated with the need for ample white space is a need to keep sentences and paragraphs short, especially when dealing with pages having a high proportion of text. One need only look to the pages of the *Reader's Digest* to see this principle enacted to mathematical precision. Publishing to a broad-based audience in reading ability and education, the editors tailor each paragraph to perfection for the sake of brevity and simplicity. This creates more white space and makes the material more psychologically inviting. If this ploy is needed for relatively light reading material such as the *Digest,* weigh the benefits to be gained in presenting the more arcane and complex technical summaries involved in a fact book.

Just as too little white space can be a problem, so can too much. It is true that professional layout artists creatively use white space extensively, especially around visuals, but they never leave such white space without rhyme or reason. A design problem common to many institutional fact books is that of limiting one page to each graph or table, which—assuming that the element need not be in a position of dominance—unnecessarily wastes space and gives a sophomoric look to the publication. Occasionally a graph or table may need to dominate the page, but one should generally avoid the single-graph-per-page syndrome. A forté of desktop publishing programs is the ability not only to mix textual and graphic elements, but also to shrink (or enlarge) graphic elements or to manipulate the size and spacing of the text to maintain balance or make it all fit neatly on the page. To ignore these capabilities is to ignore some of the chief benefits of DTP software. Figure 4.1 demonstrates how a number of elements can be fit onto a single page and still adhere to the principles of balance and variability. Take care, however, to avoid the appearance of clutter. Indeed, there is a fine line between cluttered pages and getting it all in economically.

Custom Design. A fact book should be customized to fit the personality of the institution and to meet its special needs. Organization, for example, might follow one's mission statement, with each chapter focusing on an institutional function or objective. This organization might be particularly helpful if the institution is about to undergo the self-study process. At least organize the chapters in some logical fashion that appeals to the college planners. CACC uses a conventional organization scheme in the presentation of its fact book, using the following sections:

Figure 4.1. The Pursuit of Balance, Variability, and Economy

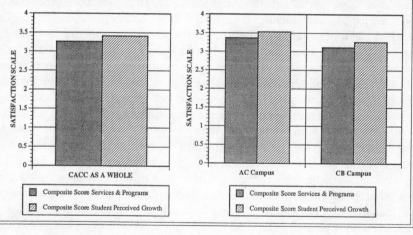

Results of CACC's
1995-96 Graduating Student Survey

Perhaps no other group of students can better assess the strengths and weaknesses of a college than those who have successfully persevered the rigors of attaining a degree. Because Central Alabama Community College is dedicated to providing the best possible learning experience for its students and the community, the assessment of graduating students has been established as an on-going tool for measuring institutional effectiveness.

Since 1993 the Office of Institutional Research has asked graduates to complete a questionnaire consisting of 64 multiple-choice items. Section A (or page 1) of the questionnaire is related to *"College Services & Programs,"* while Section B (or p. 2) is related to *"Areas of Personal Growth"* during their enrollment. These surveys are provided to potential graduates as they apply for graduation.

The completed surveys are then forwarded to the Institutional Research Office to be tallied, analyzed, and published. As a result of these efforts this past year, a total of 181 surveys were completed by those making application for graduation: 95 from the Alexander City Campus and 86 from the Childersburg Campus (see column graph next page).

The overall college results can be reduced to one composite average and graphed as in the first of the two figures below. Similarly, results can be shown as a composite average by campus, as in the second bar chart. The two charts on the next page graphically depict relative levels of graduate satisfaction with respect to *"College Services & Programs"* (Section A) and *"Areas of Personal Growth"* (Section B) during their enrollment. The composite response to each question number is graphed, and differences between the composite CACC response and response by campus can be examined. Keys to the individual questions are available in the Research Office.

CACC AS A WHOLE

AC Campus   CB Campus

Composite Score Services & Programs

Composite Score Student Perceived Growth

Background and General Information
The Service Area
Admissions and Other Student-Related Information
Student Enrollment Patterns
Degrees Conferred and Graduating Student Data
Student Activities
Staffing and Academic Information
Financial Information
Physical Facilities
Special Programs

Any logical organization plan should serve well as long as the final product offers, through the presentation of descriptive, historical, and comparative data, a terse but comprehensive view of the institution for the current year or for previous years, analyzes trends over a recent span of years, and compares the college to other similar institutions (Hackett, 1994).

As for page orientation, there is no dictate requiring fact books to use the vertical or portrait view; it just seems that way. At least one of the community colleges in Alabama (Calhoun State) regularly uses the horizontal or landscape orientation consistently throughout its fact book, being an advantage when extensively portraying wide drawings or double-sized tables. The landscape page orientation, however, demands careful and creative use of white space.

Another way to personalize one's fact book is through occasional use of the institution's logo (perhaps alongside the college's organizational chart), the school's mascot image (accompanying sports information), or any popular campus icon (such as bell tower or library silhouette). If the school uses a specific font with its logo (at CACC, that font happens to be *Friz Quadrata Bold*), buy a commercial version of that font and install it on the desktop computers used to design the fact book and other college publications. Use the logo sparingly and appropriately throughout, accompanying it with the special font for special titles or sidebars.

The fact book cover should be as carefully planned and designed as its contents, and offers considerable opportunity for innovation and custom designing. Depending on the fact book image and the spirit to be conveyed, creative use can be made of color blends, cut-through titles, and embossed or raised letter styles. Overlapped photographs, appropriate drawings suggesting the statistical nature of the publication, and of course, the school logo, can be used to advantage here. Choose from a variety of paper stock. Different bindings using colored wire or plastic can be used to highlight school colors or special themes. Whatever the result, the cover should be dignified and uncluttered.

In the back of the fact book some colleges include a clip and return evaluation form along with a brief appeal for feedback, providing a practical testimonial to the assessment spirit of the research office. Another occasional addition to the back of a fact book is a blank page (usually topped with suggestive clip art and a *Notes* heading) to be used for personal notations. Especially in large fact books or those having extensive readership, the inclusion of a topical index is often useful. An index can usually be generated by the software. However, because it requires constant attention throughout the assembly of the publication, it is often less troublesome to manually list and electronically alphabetize the headings and page numbers during the final stages of production.

Finally, to avoid an unprofessional pamphlet look to the fact book, the publication design should use both sides of the page. Such two-page spreads always require even-numbered pages on the left and odd-numbered pages on the right. A title page for a new chapter will conventionally be on an odd-numbered page, even if it requires a left-handed blank page to do so. Preliminary pages (title page, acknowledgments, table of contents, and so on) are usually numbered with small Roman numerals to set them apart from the body of the fact book.

Graphics. The extensive use of visuals is common to fact books because graphics provide an economical method of communicating numbers and the relationships among them. Within text, numbers get lost easily, or at best appear secondary to any auxiliary information being communicated within the sentence. One way to accentuate their prominence is to place such numerical information in tables or lists, thereby presenting the data in a clear, straightforward way. Rectangles of varying line widths and use of various degrees of filled gray shading can further highlight the table or list, if desired. The best way, however, to make numbers quickly and effectively jump to life and communicate otherwise hidden relationships is through the use of a chart or graph. In some cases, it may still be desirable to include a table listing the data points (for example, scores, or dollars) because although numerical relationships may be revealed evocatively through the graph or chart, the individual data points may be obscured.

Minimal effort and creativity can sometimes dramatically improve the software's default chart or graphic. Simply changing the style or size of the default font, modifying the size or shading patterns of rectangles, or adding or deleting a shadow can often improve their appearance. For example, instead of using plain vertical bars in a bar chart summarizing an inventory of audiovisual equipment, some fact book designers may choose a graphics program and clip art package to paste in bars of televisions stacked on top of each other. Some judgment and restraint needs to be exercised, however, because an unnecessarily glitzy or cute appearance may sometimes result. It is important to experiment, using a variety of methods to effectively transmit or highlight the information critical to fact book success at the institution in question.

Proper resizing of graphics is an effective means of avoiding the one-graph-per-page syndrome criticized earlier. Why not have two, three, or even four related charts appropriately balanced on one page instead of stretching them out over several pages? Always consider size reduction or expansion depending upon the importance of the visual and its relationship to its components on the page. To resize charts or other visuals, study the software manual to see how proper resizing can be done without distorting perspective or decreasing image quality.

Cropping and silhouetting graphic elements eliminate background distraction and emphasize important areas of the page. With the same resolve with which one edits paragraphs to weed out unnecessary verbiage or rewords phrases more effectively, one should also cut out or otherwise highlight the appropriate parts of any visual. Whether it be a photograph, drawing, or ready-made software chart, a visual can often be improved with proper cropping or embellishment, depending on the importance of the whole and its components. Certain parts (legends, titles, sidebars, and so on) sometimes need to be eliminated altogether.

Clip art needs to be used sparingly and selectively. For example, mixing clip art styles within a publication should probably be avoided. Propriety is also a factor. Perhaps the mascot image or the robed graduate caricature looked appropriate in the college's brochure, but is too cartoonish for serious use in the fact book. Use clip art too often and it becomes a distraction rather than an accentuating device. At worst, excessive or inappropriate use can cause a fact book to look unprofessional.

To use clip art effectively, one should have an ample variety available from which to choose. Each school or department should develop its own collection of clip art according to its needs or emphases. It can be purchased and collected through clip art services (either on disk or as scannable hardcopy) or as ready-made collections. The CD technology now affords colleges the opportunity to amass vast clip art collections both economically and conveniently. Low-cost scanners (either the small handheld or more elaborate flatbed models) provide schools the capability to instantly scan customized clip art from many outside sources as long as copyrights are not infringed.

Fact book editors without access to all the fancy technology should know that even in the most computerized operation, it often becomes necessary (sometimes desirable) to resort to the old manual cutting and pasting routine. (Yes, I mean with scissors and rubber cement or cellophane tape!) And the office copier can increase or decrease image size as readily as the most sophisticated personal computer.

Textual Concerns Within a Fact Book

The appropriate selection, formatting, placement, and alignment of text elements throughout any publication is crucial to eye appeal and readability, yet many tricks of the publishing trade are unappreciated or unknown to the general reading public.

Typefaces—Which Fonts to Use and Why. Many fonts are usually available in the DTP font menus: Times, Courier, Helvetica, Zapf Chancery, Bookman, New Century Schoolbook, Palatino, Avant Garde, and others. When publishing a fact book, less is more. Limit the use of different type faces to primarily two fonts, not counting special purpose ones such as symbols, the font associated with the college logo, or other specialty fonts. Why? Because at best, use of too many fonts may provide a garish or confused look to the text. At worst, it may give the page a carnival or ransom-note appearance. This is not to say, however, that one cannot use other styles (like bold, italic, or underline) in the fact book. That is another matter, and is acceptable as long as those styles are used sparingly, consistently, and remain commensurate with one's purpose. Also, to attain a published instead of a typewritten look, try to avoid monospaced fonts such as *Courier* and *Monaco*.

It is probably safer to limit oneself to one serif-styled font for body text and one sans serif font for display and headline fonts. Serif fonts (Bookman, Courier, New Century Schoolbook, Palatino, Times, Zapf Chancery, and so on) are easy to read in situations where the individual text characters are small, compressed, or en masse, such as in a paragraph. This easy readability is due to the serifs, or strokes, at the ends of each letterform. The little curlicues and curvatures at the tops and bottoms of the individual characters of these fonts don't serve to merely make a font look fancy; rather, serifs guide the eye along the printed line, increasing legibility.

Sans serif fonts (Avant Garde, Helvetica, Helvetica Narrow, and so on) are sometimes called display fonts because they are particularly suited for large type (headings and titles, for example). The individual characters are designed with relatively straight edges or unadorned curves. For readability, they are well adapted to spreadsheets and charts. They give a clean and modern look to text—provided the text or characters are limited in quantity (for example, a headline).

Literally thousands of typefaces are available. Be consistent; the choices of typeface for headlines, subheads, and body text should be generally the same from page to page. The owner's manuals that accompany computers or printers often have sections devoted to fonts—check there for helpful information. As a matter of personal choice, I prefer the Times font in size 10 or 12 point for body text (maybe using 9 or 10 point for indented lists or numbered subparagraphs), reserving Helvetica styles for bolder headlines, usually in 14 or 18 point, with subheads using Helvetica bold size 12 point.

Type Styles. For real textual emphasis, use highlighted text sparingly. As indicated earlier, it is perfectly acceptable to use and occasionally mix type styles such as italic, bold, underlining, and so forth, but such use can easily be overdone. One should deviate from the plain style only for effect; deviating too often or inconsistently not only confuses the reader but also ruins visual appeal. The all caps style is included in this admonishment. Occasional use to emphasize words or phrases is fine, but the all caps style grades poor on the readability index, particularly if used en masse. (Even OCR scanners have a tough time reading characters in the all caps style.) USE ALL CAPS SPARINGLY!

Another way to make one's text look professionally typefaced is to avoid using a single hyphen, or even double hyphens, for a dash. The manual accompanying the DTP software on any PC should explain how to create em-dashes (— instead of - or --) appropriately. On the Mac, for example, one holds the shift and option keys down while pressing the hyphen key. In the same sense, try to avoid use of the generic typewriter version of quotation marks and apostrophes (" '), using instead the so-called smart quotes ("" ') available as an option in most software packages.

Text Alignment and Formatting. One of the major gains to be made in moving up to word processing in DTP is the simplicity and speed with which paragraphs and other textual elements can be modified to achieve the desired visual effect. Such experimentation was simply not feasible on the typewriter. Indeed, most text alignment problems stem from typewriter habits. On a typewriter (depending on whether it used pica or elite type), an inch was exactly ten or twelve characters or spaces, respectively. An *I* took up as much space as a *W*. This is not so on the personal computer. Unless one chooses to consistently use some plain monospaced typeface such as *Courier* or *Monaco,* all letters are proportionately spaced. The only effective way to get text elements aligned properly is with the electronic rulers.

A cardinal rule for any DTP word processing: *Use the ruler to adjust the margin or tab points in order to carefully align text*—instead of using the space bar or indiscriminately tapping on the tab bar. The reason for this becomes obvious when one must later convert the text of a particular document to a different font or text size. If one has used the space bar or entered meaningless multiple tabs for alignment, the resulting conversion reveals huge gaps within the paragraphs and tables, with no corresponding alignment whatsoever. Although it may have been aligned using the default font, the document will first require extensive removal of all the spaces and unnecessary tabs, and then the substitution of the appropriate tabs and ruler settings. Here, time waste is massive, and the proscription cannot be overstated. If the ruler had been used originally, only slight ruler adjustments would have been necessary.

Consequently, DTP users should study their software manuals to learn how to use their electronic rulers to quickly and routinely adjust to the needs of each paragraph or each table. Here are several tips to avoid extensive time waste in editing and refining the fact book.

Distinguish among the four different types of tabs: left-aligned, center-aligned, right-aligned, and decimal tabs, especially for use in complex tables. These tabs are usually graphically depicted on the ruler.

Use hanging paragraphs (where the word-wrap feature automatically aligns neatly at the desired point) to advantage. All that is usually required is to select the affected paragraphs, then slide the margin markers of the ruler to the appropriate points. Refrain from using the space bar to align the second line.

For speed and efficiency, learn to copy and paste rulers into the document. Most word processing programs allow for this. Once a particular paragraph style has been defined, it is not necessary to laboriously repeat the process for each similar paragraph. Some programs allow the creation of custom styles or palettes. Other programs may use *macros* (a replaying of computer recorded key strokes and mouse movements). Whatever the method, it should be mastered.

When providing lists, give the text more eye appeal and improve readability by subordinating ensuing elements like those discussed in the following paragraphs. Bring in both the left and right margins a bit. Reduce the font size. Either number the subordinate elements or use any of several types of *bullet* styles to set them apart from the normal flow of text.

For variety and further eye appeal make subordinating elements several point sizes smaller.

When the element runs to a second line, the ruler should be adjusted to provide the automatic indent or overhang. Again, don't use the space bar or tab key to do this. Learn to use the hanging indent tool on the paragraph ruler to line up the left side. (*Warning:* Justified paragraphs cannot be used in such subordinating elements, else the left-side alignment of bullets will not align properly with the text. A ragged right-hand margin is necessary.)

Use double-spacing between subordinating elements. This, too, aids eye appeal, as do the slightly reduced left and right margins.

Widows *and* orphans *are technical, typographic terms relating to how a paragraph begins or ends at the top or bottom of a page (and sometimes columns) of text—and they are to be avoided.* A page should not end with only the first line of a new paragraph at the bottom (a widow). Edit the previous paragraph to be a bit shorter or longer, or simply skip a space and begin the new paragraph on the next page. Similarly, a page should not begin with only one line of a paragraph from the previous page (an orphan). Avoid both situations. Have the copy rewritten, or perhaps add or delete a word or two to force fit, as needed.

Justified text (block style) is not always appropriate, and in fact, its choice is often inappropriate. This is probably because justified paragraphs were almost impossible to achieve on typewriters, but it is so readily done on a word processor that people assume it is the professional preference. A look at many of the mainstream periodicals reveals a preference for ragged right-hand margins, especially in multicolumn periodicals. Why? With justified text, unless one writes all across the page and uses a small font size, annoying gaps will appear between words and perhaps letters will appear too close together. Glaring examples of this often occur in newspapers. "Furthermore, when the space between the words becomes greater than the space between the lines, it creates what are called 'rivers' running through the type" (Williams, 1990, p. 51) and this, too, distracts the reader and makes for poor readability.

Finally, encourage the typing staff to consult the software manual to master whatever keyboard shortcuts exist (called macros, control keys, and so on) for those actions and redundant keystrokes most frequently used. This time invested will reap much savings in time and frustration when the fact book deadlines are most critical.

Conclusion

Fact book design and layout is a way to increase readability and user-friendliness among general readership. Hardware and software configurations, principles of balance and design, effective use of white space, customized design strategies, placement and modification of graphics, and use of various textual strategies are all important components.

The advent of desktop publishing places the seemingly complex technology of the publishing profession at the fingertips of most professionals in the workplace. Whether this professional capability results in commensurably professional published products is another matter altogether.

It is just as important for educators to clearly and effectively communicate the facts and figures of their collegiate circumstances to their colleagues and constituents as it is for those in corporate America to clearly and effectively hawk their wares in the marketplace. True, college research staffs have traditionally dealt with numbers—and have not been trained to think as designers or publishers. But isn't it appropriate that we, in educational research, set the example of not only mastering the new technology, but fully exploiting its capabilities?

Few educators have enjoyed the luxury of a typography or publishing background. Between number crunching and proposal writing, many of us in institutional research have been too distracted searching for the on/off button to our assigned PC to venture too far beyond our comfortable realm. However, the bibliography following this chapter, taken in large part from Roger Parker's *Make-Over Book,* in addition to those excellent references already cited, provides ample opportunity for individual study to nourish the fledgling publishing genius in us all.

References

Aldus Corporation. "Articles: Spacing Between Letters, Words, and Lines of Text." *Reference Manual—Version 4.0 for Use with Apple Macintosh Computers.* Seattle, Wash.: Aldus Corporation, 1990.

Apple Computer. "All About Fonts." *LaserWriter IINT/NTX Owner's Guide.* Cupertino, Calif.: Apple Corporation, 1988.

Hackett, E. R. "Linking Institutional Research, Planning, and Budgeting: The Key to Institutional Effectiveness." Institutional Research Workshop, Auburn University, Auburn, Ala., May 1994.

Hansberry, K. (ed.). *1995 Fact Book.* John C. Calhoun State Community College, 1995. (Associate Dean's Office, P.O. Box 2216, Decatur, AL 35609–2216)

Kramer, F. *Desktop Publishing Success.* Homewood, Ill.: Irwin, 1991.

Parker, R. C. *The Make-Over Book: 101 Design Solutions for Desktop Publishing.* Chapel Hill, N.C.: Ventana Press, 1989.

Williams, R. *The Mac Is Not a Typewriter.* Berkeley, Calif.: Peachpit Press, 1990.

Selected Bibliography and Resources

Adobe Systems, Inc. *The Adobe Type Catalog.* Palo Alto, Calif.: Adobe Systems, 1987.

Beach, M. *Editing Your Newsletter: A Guide to Writing, Design and Production.* Portland, Ore.: Coast to Coast Books, 1982.

Beaumont, M. *Type: Design, Color, Character & Use.* Cincinnati, Ohio: North Light, 1987.

Bly, R. W. *The Copywriter's Handbook: A Step-By-Step Guide to Writing Copy that Sells.* New York: Dodd, Mead, 1986.

Brigham, N. *How To Do Leaflets, Newsletters and Newspapers.* New York: Hastings House, 1982.

Carter, R., Day, B., and Meggs, P. *Typographic Design: Form and Communication*. New York: Van Nostrand Reinhold, 1985.

Craig, J. *Designing with Type*. New York: Watson-Guptill, 1980.

Danuloff, C., and McClelland, D. *The Typefaces of Desktop Publishing*. Boulder, Colo.: Publishing Resources, 1987.

Fenton, E. *Canned Art: Clip Art for the Macintosh*. Berkeley, Calif.: Peachpit Press, 1992.

Gedney, K., and Fultz, P. *The Complete Guide to Creating Successful Brochures*. Westbury, N.Y.: Asher-Gallant, 1988.

Gosney, M., and Dayton, L. *Making Art on the Macintosh II*. Glenview, Ill.: Scott, Foresman, 1989.

Holmes, N. *Designer's Guide to Creating Charts & Diagrams*. New York: Watson-Guptill, 1984.

Hudson, H. P. *Publishing Newsletters: A Complete Guide to Markets, Editorial Content, Design, Printing, Subscriptions, Management, and Much More*. New York: Scribner's, 1982.

Hurlburt, A. *The Grid*. New York: Van Nostrand Reinhold, 1982.

Kelly, K. (ed.). *Sign Communication Tools for the Information Age: A Whole Earth Catalog*. Berkeley, Calif.: Whole Earth Access, 1988.

Kleper, M. L. *The Illustrated Handbook of Desktop Publishing and Typesetting*. Blue Ridge Summit, Pa.: Tab Books, 1987.

Middleton, T. *A Desktop Publisher's Guide to Pasteup: A Do-It-Yourself Guide to Preparing Camera-Ready Pasteups and Mechanicals*. Colorado Springs, Colo.: Plusware, 1987.

Nelson, R. P. *The Design of Advertising*. Dubuque, Iowa: Wm. C. Brown, 1985.

Nelson, R. P. *Publication Design*. Dubuque, Iowa: Wm. C. Brown, 1987.

Makuta, D., and Lawrence, W. F. *The Complete Desktop Publisher*. Greensboro, N.C.: "Compute!" Publications, 1986.

Pattison, P. *How to Design a Nameplate: A Guide for Art Directors and Editors*. Chicago: Ragan Communications, 1982.

Perfect, C., and Rookledge, G. *Rookledge's International Typefinder: The Essential Handbook of Typeface Recognition & Selection*. Glen Cove, N.Y.: PBC International, 1986.

Pickens, J. E. *The Copy-to-Press Handbook: Preparing Words and Art for Print*. New York: Wiley, 1985.

Romano, F. J. *The Type Encyclopedia: A User's Guide to Better Typography*. New York: Bowker, 1984.

Seybold, J., and Dressler, F. *Publishing from the Desktop*. New York: Bantam Books, 1987.

Swann, A. *How to Understand and Use Design and Layout*. Cincinnati, Ohio: North Light, 1987.

Tufte, E. R. *The Visual Display of Quantitative Information*. Cheshire, Conn.: Graphics Press, 1987.

Webb, R. A. (ed.). *The Washington Post Deskbook on Style*. New York: McGraw-Hill, 1978.

White, A. *How to Spec Type*. New York: Watson-Guptill, 1987.

White, I. V. *Designing for Magazines: Common Problems, Realistic Solutions*. New York: Bowker, 1982.

White, I. V. *Mastering Graphics: Design and Production Made Easy*. New York: Bowker, 1983.

White, J. V. *Editing by Design: A Guide to Effective Word-and-Picture Communication for Editors and Designers*. New York: Bowker, 1982.

White, J. V. *18 Ready to Use Grids for Standard 8½" x 11" Pages*. Arlington, Va.: National Composition Service.

Associations and Seminars

Dynamic Graphics & Education Foundation (workshops)
6000 North Forest Park Drive
P.O.Box 1901
Peoria, IL 61656–1901

National Association of Desktop Publishers
P.O. Box 508, Kenmore Station
Boston, MA 02215–9998

Newsletter Association
1401 Wilson Boulevard, Suite 403
Arlington, VA 22209

Performance Seminar Group (workshops)
204 Strawberry Hill Avenue
Norwalk, CT 06851

Promotion Perspectives (workshops)
1955 Pauline Boulevard, Suite 1OOA
Ann Arbor, MI 48103

The Newsletter Clearinghouse
44 West Market Street
Rhinebeck, NY 12572

Newsletters

Font & Function: The Adobe Type Catalog, Adobe Systems, Inc., Mountain View, CA. Quarterly.
How Magazine, F & W Publications, Cincinnati, OH. Bimonthly.
ITC Desktop, International Typographic Corporation, Hammarskjold Plaza, New York, NY. Bimonthly.
Newsletter Design, Newsletter Clearing House, P.O. Box 301, Rhinebeck, NY. Monthly.
PC Publishing, Hunter Publications, Des Plaines, IL. Monthly.
Personal Publishing, Renegade Publications, Ithaca, NY. Monthly.
Print: America's Graphic Design Magazine, RC Publications, New York, NY. Bimonthly.
Publish! PCW Communications, San Francisco, CA. Monthly.
Step-By-Step Electronic Design: The How-To Newsletter for Electronic Designers and Desktop Publishers, Dynamic Graphics, P.O. Box 1901, Peoria, IL 61656–1901. Monthly.
The Page, Box 14493, Chicago, IL 60614. Monthly.
Type World, Typeworld Publications, Salem, NH. Monthly.
U&LC, International Typographic Publications, Salem, NH. Monthly.
Verbum: The Journal of Computer Aesthetics, P.O. Box 15439, San Diego, CA 92115. Quarterly.

JAMES A. THOMPSON is director of research and planning at Central Alabama Community College.

Electronic fact books have been produced by institutional research offices with varying success. This chapter illustrates what is required and a process for creating a successful electronic fact book.

Electronic Fact Books: Turning Atoms into Bits

Robert F. Daly, Dennis W. Viehland

Other chapters in this issue discuss the purpose, uses, roles, and development of fact books. Much of what is said in those chapters applies equally well to electronic fact books. Just like a paper fact book, an electronic fact book can be an incredibly valuable information resource for a college or university. Unlike a paper fact book, an electronic collection of data can always be up to date, access underlying layers of information, and, at its best, be customized to meet the needs of each user or group of users.

In his book *Being Digital,* Nicholas Negroponte (1995) points out that the fundamental particle for the information age is not the atom, but the bit. We read magazines, newspapers, journals, and fact books (atoms), but the value is in the information (bits). As more and more of the world's *infostructure* is built, much of the information we consume (text, images, sound, video) is being delivered by bits. *Being digital* means that information providers (publishers, marketing professionals, institutional researchers) recognize that bits are radically different from atoms (weightless, easily reproduced, shipped anywhere, infinite in supply) and adjust their delivery mechanisms accordingly. Bits, not atoms, are the delivery mechanism of the information age, and those unwilling to adapt to this new age will be as extinct as the hunters and gatherers of an earlier age.

A large number and variety of electronic fact books have been produced over the past twenty years. In fact, some institutional research (IR) professionals and computing specialists have created three or four different electronic fact books during their careers, including one of the authors. The developers of electronic fact books usually began construction because they believed that electronic fact books would be much used and would provide the needed value added over paper fact books. They expected them to be successful. However, the success has been varied. Far too many electronic fact books, which took hundreds of hours to design and develop, are now collecting dust next to their paper cousins. What happened? The primary reason is that far too many electronic fact books are just paper fact books displayed electronically. They do not provide the necessary value added compared to paper fact books that is needed for success. What is required to create a electronic fact book that has the necessary value added? That is the theme of this chapter.

What Is an Electronic Fact Book?

As previously defined, a fact book can be considered to be a collection of organized facts. In its simplest and most common form, an electronic fact book is a paper fact book displayed on a computer screen. These on-line paper fact books feature static data with set formats and are simply an electronic reproduction of a printed page. Electronic fact books of this kind are the simplest to build and are relatively inexpensive. Most IR offices already have the resources and skills necessary to construct an on-line paper fact book.

Fact books built with presentation packages, desktop publishing software, flat databases, or even Gopher software are illustrative of *on-line paper* fact books. The data structure for on-line paper fact books is typically a series of text-based tables, or simple flat databases such as spreadsheets. Slabaugh and Newsom (1991) used the UNIX shell and utilities to create a flat-file electronic fact book, called *Fast Facts,* at Ball State. Accessed by logging in to a UNIX system, *Fast Facts* is character-based and allows the user to select facts through a series of menus. Gopher and, more recently, World Wide Web (WWW) technologies drive other examples of flat-file electronic fact books. Excellent examples can be found at Boston College; Colorado State University; Florida State University; Skidmore College; Southern Illinois University; University of Arizona; University of California, Irvine; University of Colorado at Boulder; University of Ottawa; University of South Carolina; University of Texas-Pan American; and Wake Forest University. Many IR professionals have used spreadsheets to build flat-file electronic fact books. Todd Massa, while at St. Louis University, may have built the most comprehensive spreadsheet fact book, using Microsoft Excel in conjunction with Visual Basic add-ons, and the Windows Help Engine. Continuing his work at Willamette University, Massa is developing a flat-file electronic fact book that is done in MediaView and a variation of the MS Multimedia Viewer Publisher's Toolkit. MediaView and Viewer offer enhancements such as full-text indexing that will provide a fast searching capability for the user. Another spreadsheet-based electronic fact book (Gaylord and Jones, 1994) was developed at the University of Alaska at Fairbanks. This electronic fact book, which included an extensive number of macros to make it easy to use and flexible in its reporting of data, also used Microsoft Excel. The University of Alaska's fact book was rather extensive, containing ten megabytes in data. Multiple copies were available for users to access, residing on the campus and University Statewide System servers.

One of the potential disadvantages of electronic fact books is that they tend to be accessible only from a desktop computer. However, the use of personal digital assistants (PDAs) offers great potential to eliminate this restriction. A prototype PDA electronic fact book has been built by Robert Daly and Mark Herringer, of the Western Farm Credit Bank, for the Apple Newton. A PDA-based fact book is as portable as a paper-based book and retains all of the functionality and most of the advantages of a desk-based electronic fact book. This PDA electronic fact book can be downloaded from the University of Iowa's Newton FTP site.

The flat-file electronic fact book usually offers a higher degree of value than a similar paper-based book, but whether that value exceeds the additional cost of construction depends on a variety of factors including cost, availability, and use by the target audience. Although now available electronically, the data and their presentation generally remain static. An electronic fact book becomes dynamic in its organization and reporting of facts when relational database technology is used. These dynamic electronic fact books allow a user to obtain data from an information support database or data warehouse and organize and view those data in a manner that is meaningful to the user. Fact books built with client-server tools using a set of summarized and highly organized relational databases are illustrative of dynamic fact books.

Allan MacDougall, while at Southwestern College, may have produced one of the very best dynamic electronic fact books using IFPS, executive information system software from Execucom Corporation (MacDougall, 1979). Southwestern's electronic fact book was quite comprehensive, provided some *drill-down* capabilities, and served as an important decision support tool for the college's administration. Several efforts are currently underway to build dynamic fact books. Louisiana State University is building a dynamic electronic fact book using SQL to extract information from DB2, an IBM-based relational database (Hadden and Evans, 1992).

Electronic Fact Book Functions

Though different in terms of the degree of sophisticated computing technology used, both on-line, flat-file and dynamic electronic fact books serve the same functions. In an unpublished document, Michael Marentette (1995) provides an excellent list of electronic fact book functions and corresponding concerns in electronic fact book development. Marentette suggests that electronic fact books function as a campuswide information source. Any user who is interested in general information about the university can access the electronic fact book and obtain the information. It is fairly obvious, then, that the value of an electronic fact book can be increased by wide and easy access.

Marketing Tool. This is a function that many fact book developers have not fully considered. Prospective students and their parents, donors, potential faculty, and members of the public can access the electronic fact book in search of information about academic programs, the student body, and the institution and its community. The degree to which the electronic fact book will be accessed by the public needs to be addressed during its design. For example, making the fact book accessible via Gopher or the World Wide Web greatly expands the potential audience, but also impacts on presentation and data interpretation considerations (for example, will the public understand what is meant by FTEs, restricted funds, or contact hours?).

An electronic fact book can also serve as a marketing tool for the IR office. This role should not be undervalued as a method to improve (or establish) the reputation of value of the campus IR office in the institution, media, and surrounding community.

Decision Support Tool. The value of a paper-based fact book is enhanced by making it electronic, especially if the electronic fact book is connected to the underlying information support database that is used for ongoing decision support activities. The dynamic electronic fact books just described can supply the decision maker not only general static information but also levels of detailed information. Whether used by institutional executives, college and department administrators, or IR professionals, the electronic fact book can serve as a valuable analytical tool and enhance the delivery of information for decision making. Indeed, for many institutional managers a dynamic electronic fact book can be viewed as a type of decision support system (DSS).

Management Reporting Tool. An analyst in an operational office who needs general as well as very detailed information can use an electronic fact book to prepare reports that can have an impact on a college or university's operational procedures.

Electronic Fact Book Advantages

The functions listed in the previous section might apply, to varying degrees, to paper-based fact books as well. What is special about electronic fact books? What are the distinguishing characteristics offered by turning paper atoms into information bits? The advantages of being digital are as follows.

Dynamic Information. Once a fact book is published electronically, the capability for including dynamic, constantly changing information is recognized and often requested. Users now want access to quarterly, monthly, weekly, or even daily updates of budget, enrollment, and news information. An electronic fact book, especially a dynamic electronic fact book, can serve this need.

Display Format Preference. The fact book can be delivered to users in a format they prefer. Some users will want paper-based fact books, some electronic, and some both. With an electronic fact book all users can be satisfied. Build an electronic fact book and, when required, print from it a paper version to satisfy both types of users. Additionally, a dynamic electronic fact book allows users to produce customized personal paper fact books that will serve their special requirements.

The electronic fact book also allows users with different preferences for tabular data or graphics to customize the data to their liking.

Drill-Down. An electronic fact book can deliver underlying information more easily. Indeed, when built on an underlying information support database or data warehouse, the capabilities of a dynamic electronic fact book far exceed those of paper fact books.

Up-to-the-Minute Accuracy. At first it seems that fact book data rarely require such an immediate level of currency. However, few paper fact books are printed error-free. An electronic one can be corrected as errors are found. Additionally, traditional fact book data can be published only as they become available. Whenever a paper-based fact book is published it inevitably misses some reporting deadline (for example, end of fiscal year, enrollment report date). Publication of an electronic fact book becomes a continuous process, not cyclic. This allows users to develop more confidence in its accuracy and currency.

Data Format. Although not directly an advantage for the user, an active and viable electronic fact book can create an environment where data production systems (for example, the registration, ledger, personnel systems) will begin to address the data needs of analytical and decision support systems. As recommended by Hadden and Evans (1992), the production system should deposit information into the electronic fact book's information database, allowing the electronic fact book, not the operational system, to dictate the format of data.

Available Anywhere, Anytime. This used to be a valid reason for not creating an electronic fact book. Until very recently, availability anywhere and at any time was a justification for a paper-based fact book. Now the development of PDAs and expansion of the world's *infostructure* means that an electronic fact book accessible from the Internet is available anywhere at any time. Even if this is not the case for your institution today, it will be. The atoms-to-bits conversion will make it so.

Electronic Fact Book Characteristics

Not surprisingly, electronic fact books have certain characteristics that are shared with all information delivery systems, but especially DSS and EIS (executive information systems). An electronic fact book can be considered a DSS (Marentette, 1995) or part of an EIS (Glover, 1989 Hadden and Evans, 1992 and Viehland, 1989). This relationship to these management support systems is exceptionally important in terms of the design and implementation of a dynamic electronic fact book. Especially, electronic fact books should be constructed using the techniques and methods used to build DSS and EIS. Readers not familiar with management support system design should refer to Turban (1995) or Burkan (1991) for more information.

What are the distinguishing characteristics of an electronic fact book? This is an important question because it is the implementation of these characteristics that will create the necessary value added for an electronic fact book to be a success. Articles by Viehland (1989) and Slabaugh and Newsom (1991) jointly provide a comprehensive list of the characteristics of a dynamic electronic fact book. Listed in order of importance, the characteristics required of all electronic fact books follow.

Information Database or Data Warehouse. This database will not be transaction level records (such as a student's academic record), but must be a fairly comprehensive database of aggregated data. Whereas simple electronic fact books can use flat files of data, as the sophistication of the electronic fact book increases, the data file structure will also have to become more sophisticated, and eventually, relational databases will be necessary. But whatever the type of electronic fact book, it is absolutely critical that it be built on appropriate data in the appropriate type of database.

Very Fast, No Delay in Retrieving Facts. Many electronic fact books have been unsuccessful because they required the user to wait several minutes before the facts were displayed. Appropriate response time for an electronic fact book is measured in a few seconds. Fortunately, with today's increasingly faster hardware, relational databases that are indexed, and standard query tools such as SQL, quick response speed is becoming easier to achieve.

Novice-Friendly Interface. An electronic fact book should be an *everybody's information system* (EIS), not just for executives, but for everyone. Reviewing graphical user interface (GUI) development standards such as the *Human Interface Guidelines* (Apple Computer, 1987) is highly recommended before beginning the development of an electronic fact book.

Widespread Availability. This characteristic implies the choice of appropriate client software, and usually for an IR office, this implies very low cost. The desire for access to the electronic fact book from off campus has led to the use of Gopher and World Wide Web software for the electronic fact book client and TCP/IP as the networking protocol. Considering the hypertext and multimedia characteristics of the World Wide Web, it can be expected that this Internet resource will be the next focus for the development of electronic fact books.

Graphic Oriented. Graphic orientation is a feature that is highly desired but rarely implemented in an electronic fact book. Most electronic fact books that have been developed are text-based, offering few if any graphical representations of the data. Graphical features, however, can be excessive, adding little improvement in the understanding of the facts in the electronic fact book, and excessive use of graphics can severely reduce the speed of retrieving facts.

Key Word Search Feature. This feature has not been incorporated into most existing electronic fact books. However, we might expect that electronic fact books will feature fewer figures and more words. As this happens, key word search features will have obvious value for greatly improving the usefulness and value of the electronic fact book. Fortunately, search features are becoming a standard part of client application software. For example, many WWW browsers incorporate excellent search capabilities.

Implementation Readiness

How can you know whether your institution is ready for an electronic fact book? In the following paragraphs we describe three stages of readiness: not ready, moderately ready, and ready to implement an electronic fact book. No institution will match any of these stages exactly. Your college or university is likely to be a mixture of two or all three.

The stages not only give an indication of an institution's readiness to implement an electronic fact book but also provide some guidance as to steps or processes to put in place for an institution to make progress toward establishing an electronic fact book. The three stages of readiness are presented as a matrix in Table 5.1. This matrix displays the three stages in relation to the necessary components of electronic fact book development.

Not Ready to Implement an Electronic Fact Book. At this stage of readiness, a college or university should not attempt to implement an electronic fact book. It will be prone to failure. Essentially, none of the necessary electronic fact book components, listed on the left side of the figure, are in place.

In this stage, most executive managers and heads of departments do not use computers or only use them minimally for nonanalytic functions (for example, electronic mail, word processing). The desktop computers that are used by prospective fact book clients differ, and most workstations are several years old. Many of the campus computer users are frustrated by the difficulty of electronic communications because there are no networking protocol or client-server platform standards for data delivery. Prospective users of the fact book use a variety of analytical software packages (for example, spreadsheets, graphics, statistics).

Adding to the complications, institutional research is a decentralized function with departments and colleges competing with each other for the provision of data to executive management. All institutional data are held in separate databases on a variety of computers using different operating systems. Usually the ones with the best information get what they want. Requests to answer public relations inquiries, complete official reporting forms, or provide decision support usually take several days to prepare. There is minimal communication between Computing Services and the Institutional Research office. The IR staff are unfamiliar with managerial requirements for information and have little or no experience in producing a paper-based fact book. In fact, a paper-based fact book does not exist.

Moderate Readiness to Implement an Electronic Fact Book. At this stage of readiness, an institution could implement a simple flat-file electronic fact book. This is possible because a data warehouse or information support database is in place. For the most part, the data in the database are accessed

Table 5.1. Electronic Fact Book: Implementation Readiness

	Not Ready	Moderately Ready	Ready
Data	•Separate data bases •Data access by operational staff	•Data warehouse(s) •Data access by analysts, not managers	•Data warehouse(s) •Hands-on data access by managers procedures
Users	•Management rarely uses computers	•Management is interested •No executive sponsors	•Management has requested a fact book •Executive sponsor advisory committee exists
Computers/ Campus Network	•No campus network •Several years old	•Campus network in development •Mixture of new and recent computers	•Campus network is operational •Mostly new computers or plans to upgrade
Software	•No client/server software in use •No standards	•Some client/server software in use •No standard	•Campus wide client/server software •Client server software protocol standards in place
Institutional Reaearch	•Decentralized •Poor communication between IR and computing offices •IR not familiar with mgmt information needs •No experience in producing a paper fact book	•Centralized •Communication exists between IR and computing offices •IR familiar with mgmt information needs •Some experience producing a paper fact book	•Centralized •Excellent communication between IR and computing offices •IR familiar with mgmt information needs •Very experienced in producing a paper fact book
Paper fact book	•No paper fact book	•Paper fact book exists and is used	•Two types of paper fact books; senior management version with details, external version with summaries

by decision support analysts, not managers. The quality of the data is mixed, some of them are not up-to-date and in compliance with a set of consistent reporting requirements. A single authority controls database access, but no formal procedures exist. The existence of this information support database makes it possible for electronic fact book development to begin.

To aid in the potential success of electronic fact book development, several managers have asked for fact book data to be available electronically even though no executive sponsor has come forward. Many of these prospective users of the fact book have newer computers on their desks and use them for statistical or spreadsheet analysis. The users are requesting an increasing amount of data, and an institutionwide client-server platform needed to satisfy these needs has just been established and is being tested by a number of departments. Utilities for requesting data from the database servers and translating the data for use in desktop applications exist but are not well coordinated. The campus network to support this client-server environment is under development.

The IR office in this stage of readiness is a centralized function that contains an information management group that assists department heads, deans, and institutional management in obtaining the information they need. The IR office has successfully produced a paper-based fact book for several years and it is used by a variety of clients both within the institution and externally. However, the IR office and Computing Services are frequently at odds about maintenance of the data warehouse and the provision of electronic data to managers and their quality and consistency. This last issue will continue to impede further electronic fact book development.

Ready to Implement an Electronic Fact Book. At the ideal stage of readiness, every component listed in the readiness matrix is in place; thus, the necessary environment exists to implement an electronic fact book. The institution could easily and quickly move beyond simple flat-file electronic fact books and produce a dynamic-style electronic fact book. The possibility of producing an electronic fact book exists because a client-server information support database is in place and has been operating successfully for a year or more. Quality control procedures for maintaining the data integrity of the database exist, and a single authority monitors updates of the database for compliance with these procedures. Additionally, small numbers of utilities for requesting data from the database server and translating the data for use in desktop applications have been approved and are readily available.

The prospective users of the campus electronic fact book have newer computers on their desks and use them for statistical or spreadsheet analysis, as well as for graphical presentations. An advisory committee to oversee provision of data for decision support exists, is proactive and supports the development of the electronic fact book, and has the backing of the president.

In this most ready state, Institutional Research is a centralized function that is the recognized authority for the provision of information for decision support. The IR Office and Computing Services have a healthy working relationship. Several members of the IR staff have developed a keen interest in the information requirements of the senior executive team. The IR office has considerable experience producing paper fact books, and two paper-based fact books exist. Executives, deans, and department heads have an extensive and detailed administrative fact book in a three-ring binder, and regular corrections or updates are provided. An annually produced, smaller, more graphical fact book exists for distribution to external clients. Both fact books have a well-deserved reputation for reliability and accuracy.

The Seven-Day Electronic Fact Book

It is written that God created the heavens and the earth in six days. Compared to this, shouldn't the development of a prototype electronic fact book be possible in a week? Normally one would not design an electronic fact book under these conditions, only if dire circumstances required it. Realistically, the development of an electronic fact book will likely take several months. However, with careful preparation and pragmatic expectations, the institution should be able to get a prototype electronic fact book in user's hands within seven days. Following are the necessary steps in the beginning stages of electronic fact book development.

As the earlier section on institutional readiness demonstrated, the launch of an electronic fact book assumes a certain environment is in place before the development process begins. The data, hardware, network, and software must be in place and the institutional culture must be acceptable. To the greatest extent possible, pages from the existing paper-based fact book should be available, although the underlying links to the information support database may not be in place.

The people resource should be ready as well. There should be a staff group from the Institutional Research Office and Computing Services organizations. The staff group should be formed into two subgroups: a database design group and a page design group. A client advisory group composed of executives, data providers, and electronic fact book clients should exist or be assembled for this exercise.

Monday Noon. A final preparatory luncheon meeting of the staff group. The week is previewed and the specific objectives for Monday are outlined and discussed. The staff group will develop the prototype and many of its members will continue the development process after the seventh day.

Monday Afternoon. Meet with the advisory group to uncover their needs and requirements. Pages from the existing fact book are distributed as part of a questionnaire that asks about frequency of use, clarity, value of data on the page, and format. Answers are recorded on Scantron sheets for rapid generation of results. Sample reports, file formats, and data definitions are solicited from the group. If the group is large, smaller groups are formed for detailed discussion. If a group-decision-room facility is available it is used to brainstorm ideas and to prevent opinion leaders (for example, executives) from exerting too much control.

A mixture of exercises is used to discover what aspects of the paper-based fact book should be kept and to identify new data, pages, and graphics that should be included. Note especially that the existing fact book can be a good starting point, but simply converting paper to bits does not add enough value to justify the electronic version. Examining different options for data delivery helps avoid *paving the cow paths,* an all-too-common problem when redesigning manual or paper systems into electronic formats. At all times be realistic. Making wish lists should be avoided and ranking exercises should accompany any list of things to be done.

After an intensive advisory group meeting, the staff group reconvenes to analyze and summarize the meeting. A strong leader manages this meeting to ensure that it stays on track with a goal of establishing the week's priorities. The quantitative data (that is, client feedback about current fact book pages) and sample materials are distributed to the appropriate staff.

Tuesday Morning. Study the results of the meetings. Look for similarities in the data formats, themes in what the users were saying, and key dimensions in the data (that is, time, categories, historical versus actual, who uses what data). Much of the next two days will focus on data: where to get them, how to store them, and how to format them for presentation. A good data design will make that task easier, and that is the goal of the evening's work.

Tuesday Afternoon. The staff group splits up. The database design team begins to create a database using the data design sketched out on the previous evening. The page design team begins revising the existing fact book pages and creating new pages based on the input from Tuesday's meeting. Because one of the most powerful features of a dynamic electronic fact book is drill-down tables (tables with more detailed data that are connected to summary data tables), much of this day will be spent creating these underlying tables and pages.

Wednesday Morning. The database design continues with the focus on getting access to the data that are necessary. Most of this should be in the data warehouse, but other sources, including the potential collection of the data from departments, also need to be considered. The page design team extends their work by creating graphics that underlie the tables that were built in the morning. Problems, limits, and data definitions are noted. Where necessary, data for these graphics are typed in, rather than wait for the database team to provide the links.

Wednesday Afternoon. Bring the database and page design teams together to discuss progress, problems, and final delivery of the fact book. What are the most important tasks to get a bare-bones prototype (even without all data links) working by Friday morning? Specify precisely what tasks have to be done today and what can be put off until later.

Thursday Morning. Resolve any existing data problems, get some real data from the database, and begin to display real fact book pages. By the end of the day a small electronic fact book of approximately ten pages with underlying detailed tables and graphics should be ready for sharing with the advisory group.

Thursday Afternoon. Meet with the advisory group again and show them the results of the efforts from the past two days. Again ask them to rate and rank the prototype pages that have been developed. Share with them plans of what will be in place by Monday and what are priorities for development past this exercise. Discuss data definitions with them to confirm that they are interpreting the data in the tables correctly.

Friday Morning. Make the format and data changes that were suggested in the Thursday afternoon meeting. Based on direction from the Thursday meeting as well as a test of the database design, create an additional three to five pages.

Friday Afternoon. Make a formal demonstration of the electronic fact book to the advisory group. Carefully note every suggested change. Thank them for their advice and contributions.

Weekend. If Friday was a complete success, relax. Most likely some members of the staff group will be spending some time during this period getting the pieces to work together properly.

Monday Morning. Show the electronic fact book prototype to a larger group of clients and the executive management. Explain future development plans. Celebrate with a well-deserved gourmet lunch. Tomorrow a smaller staff group continues the work that began during this week as the institution moves toward achieving a complete electronic fact book.

Summary

An electronic fact book will rarely replace the paper-based fact book, at least in the short term. A fact book is published for many purposes, including public relations for external audiences, as an historical record, and as a means of providing decision support to departmental, college, and executive managers.

A paper-based fact book may fill the public-relations and historical-records purposes, but planning and decision making require access to a wider range of current and historical information in a more manageable format. The act of committing facts to paper makes the resulting paper-based fact book static and selective. A more dynamic and fluid approach to fact book data is needed for planning and decision-support activities. In this role the electronic fact book excels.

Even though electronic fact books were developed nearly twenty years ago, few have been judged successful by the *value-added* standard proposed here. They have not been able to serve the functions desired, nor have they been developed with the characteristics viewed as essential to the electronic fact book. In some measure, it seems reasonable to conclude that electronic fact books have suffered this fate due to a lack of computing technology. Most IR professionals have experienced the frustration of trying to provide highly summarized information in a matter of a few seconds from a sequential database containing tens of thousand of records. The reality is that it takes, at a minimum, several minutes: much too long for an electronic fact book user to wait. But with many of the recent advances and increases in access speed of relational technology, and the more frequent use of industry standard HTML (Hyper Text Markup Language) in conjunction with the World Wide Web, retrieval of data from electronic fact books will increase in terms of speed, have wider availability and accessibility, and have built-in search features. It will then be up to the IR professional to determine the type of electronic fact book to develop and whether or not the college or university is ready. Institutional readiness may not be a question of whether to build an electronic fact book, but simply a matter of when.

References

Apple Computer, Inc. *Human Interface Guidelines: The Apple Desktop Interface.* Menlo Park, Calif.: Addison-Wesley, 1987.

Burkan, W. C. *Executive Information Systems: From Proposal Through Implementation.* New York: Van Nostrand Reinhold, 1991.

Gaylord, T. A., and Jones, M. "A Linked Planning and Budgeting System Using a Cross-Platform Multi-Media Data Base." Paper presented at the 34th annual forum of the Association for Institutional Research, New Orleans, May 1994.

Glover, R. H. "Decision Support/Executive Systems at the University of Hartford." *Cause/Effect,* Fall 1989, *12* (3).

Hadden C. M., and Evans, B. F. "The Electronic Fact Book: The Foundation for a University Wide Decision Support System." Paper presented at CAUSE 92, Dallas, Tex., Dec. 1992.

MacDougall, A. "The Southwestern College Fact Book." Paper presented at the Southern California Association for Institutional Research, Chula Vista, Calif., 1979.

Marentette, M. "Electronic Fact Book and the University Environment." Unpublished paper, University Planning Office, McGill University, 1995.

Negroponte, N. *Being Digital.* New York: Knopf, 1995.

Paller, A., and Laska, R. *The EIS Book: Information Systems for Top Managers.* Homewood, Ill.: Dow Jones-Irwin, 1990.

Slabaugh, K., and Newsom, H. W. "Fast Facts: An Online Campus Information System." *Cause/Effect,* Spring 1991, *14* (1).

Turban, E. *Decisions Support Systems and Expert Systems.* (4th ed.) London: Prentice Hall, 1995.

Viehland, D. W. "Executive Information Systems in Higher Education." *Cause/Effect,* Fall 1989, *12* (3).

ROBERT F. DALY is director of analytical studies and information management at the University of California, Irvine.

DENNIS W. VIEHLAND is senior lecturer in the Department of Information Systems at Massey University, Auckland, New Zealand.

A description of one institutional researcher's use of a fact book with some practical advice on how to make the fact book meet a variety of institutional needs and the needs of a variety of users.

The Fact Book at Work and Play: Strategies for Use

Ann W. Tomlinson

The trouble with our times is that the future is not what it used to be.
—Paul Valery (1987, p. 10)

Fact books have been a significant annual part of my career for the past eight years. When I started, the University of Southern Mississippi (USM) *Fact Book* was issued as a three-ring binder kind of thing with pages distributed one at a time during the year, primarily as a cost-saving device. Although there were six or seven phone lines in the office ringing most of the day, most questions were general and routine fact-book-type questions. It was difficult to respond quickly, but the system somehow worked, albeit ineffectively and inefficiently. As I learned more about peer institutions and their fact books, we began to rethink and redesign our fact book until it has now evolved into a publication widely used as a planning reference, for institutional trend analysis, and as a public relations document. In fact, last year the *Fact Book* went into a second printing.

Because there was no budget for the first printed USM *Fact Book*, I sold the copies to other units and offices at the university, which resulted in a budgetary increase and, more important, established the need for such a document. Significantly, it also created a loyal following of *Fact Book* subscribers and users. The telephone still rings incessantly, but the calls received now raise more complex questions, primarily because routine information for the first level questions is readily available. Among the frequent accolades we receive for the *Fact Book* are those that sound like these: "I always check The *Fact Book* first" (an assistant vice president, Academic Affairs); "The *Fact Book* is a very useful tool" (dean of Admissions, Recruitment, and Orientation); "The *Fact Book* is full of great general information" (new employee, Development Office); "The *Fact Book* is a wonderful resource. I appreciate having it on my desk" (dean of the College of Arts).

We've come a long way with our *Fact Book,* but are we where we want to be now? In a word, no, and for several critical reasons. First, as the quality of the *Fact Book* continues to improve, expectations for greater detail and for instant information are increasing. Second, the mission of the office has now broadened to include planning and assessment responsibilities, giving the *Fact Book* greater utility. Given the new focus of planning and assessment in higher education and at USM, I think the *Fact Book* should include five-year trend data and performance indicators of departmental productivity. In addition, the *Fact Book* audience is becoming more diverse, including not only administrators and planners but also a more technically sophisticated faculty and staff who are themselves data-driven. Our current *Fact Book* customers include local journalists, development officers, grant writers, and student and staff recruiters.

In reality, the value of a fact book can be measured by the usefulness and relevance of the information. Obviously, if the fact book is to keep pace with the advances in available information and data needs, in client sophistication, and in technology, it must respond in kind. It is our intent to make our fact books reflect, in format and style, our best efforts to keep the data relevant, useful, and easily accessible. As with all types of communication, my strategies for maintaining and enhancing the utility of the fact book are based on two considerations: the audience and the purpose or use of the information.

The Audience

In my view, there are three audience issues influencing the use of the fact book that must be considered in fact book planning and development: context, the customer, and distribution.

Context. The context of delivering information in the academic community can be dramatized by everyday events on and off campus. The nutrition conscious professional of today who orders her salad with the salad dressing on the side, "holds" the anchovies and the egg, wants no butter on the bread, and lemon in the water, but no sugar in the tea, is a good personal example. More specifically, colleagues who ask for fact book information with customized changes such as "could you reverse the columns of data?" or "could you give it to me on a diskette?" or "would you just e-mail the file?" further illustrate the point. It seems everyone wants what you have, but they want it like they want it, not exactly as you have it available.

Mass Customizing. The response to this *I want it like I want it* phenomenon is known as *mass customizing* (Davis, 1987), which simply means that people in the current environment expect to receive information in a manner and style that meets their individual needs. It also seems to describe one of several contextual phenomena in which the fact book and institutional research must operate. In addition to the mass customizing context, there are three other context issues, identified and defined by Davis (1987) as demands and expectations in the new work place (Boyett and Conn, 1991), which I think influence the development and use of the fact book: they are time, place, and value added.

Time. If there is a common issue faced by institutional researchers everywhere, it must certainly be the universal expectation of immediate turnaround time or the *zero-based* time factor. There is an expectation in the academic community that information must be available immediately and without regard to how much time the information may take to obtain. Regardless of complexity of the data, the common assumption is that institutional researchers can simply press a button to get a nice spreadsheet providing the exact information requested in precisely the necessary format required, if, for some reason, it wasn't already prepared in anticipation of the request. That expectation simply cannot be met by my shop, and I'm still looking for the IR office where it can be so they can tell me how to do it. We find, however, that our fact books do a rather good job of meeting much of the *I want it now* demand.

Place. Because faculty and others have access to PC work stations in their offices, homes, and even on the road, and can log on or call in from car, plane, home, or wherever, they expect to have access to institutional and resource databases and information regardless of where they are or what particular hardware or software they might be using. The expectation for access to available data no longer seems to have spatial limits. We have designed several fact book products (described in more detail later in the chapter) to help meet the *anyplace* needs of our clients.

Value Added. Although much of society is looking for tangible evidence of value or value added, the evidence of value, particularly among the service industries, is getting more difficult to identify. Obviously, poor service may be better than no service, but is poor service with a smile really that much better than good service without a smile? Is something done quickly really better than something done well? The value—time, information, knowledge, and so on— we add or provide through our efforts is often more intangible than tangible and often not recognized or measured by those benefiting. Educators have a strategic advantage here because we have always dealt with an intangible output or product. Because many of our IR clients have considerable information available from many other sources on-and off-line, they are looking for a place to receive information and services with extra value. Whether it be service with a smile, a human touch, or someone to assist in the process, people will gravitate toward an office that gives a little extra.

Because I view our office as a support service to the university, I think it is important that a person requesting information feel that we are helpful, efficient, and accommodating. After all, we exist to support the work of others. I always say, I want it like they want it! or, in other words, whatever format is requested is the way the report should be produced. Perhaps our customer service philosophy could be likened to the McDonald's model: customers should know what they are going to get and they should know it will be delivered quickly and with a friendly smile and in an attractive environment. Over the years, we have tried to develop the format of the fact book so that users know what they are getting, they get it in a timely fashion, it is good quality (a higher quality than McDonald's, I think), and they can expect good service when they request it.

In combination, the mass customizing, time, place, and value-added contextual considerations work together (and sometimes in opposition) to create a very complex information-rich environment. Although data and requests for data are ever increasing, so too is the complexity of the issues and the data and the expectation (demand) for quality of service. Within this complicated environment for institutional research, I have learned to *under promise* but to *over deliver* as much as possible.

The Customer. There are three distinct customer groups in our IR audience today. Borrowing from Stanley Davis (1987), I refer to them as the selective, service-sensitive, and self-service-oriented.

Selective Customers. I think most everyone in our modern society falls into the selective category because selective customers are those who place a high value on speed, quality product, and quality service. I assume that everyone who is in the academic environment expects efficient service and accurate, professional reports. However, in addition to these selective expectations, customers also display characteristics that further sort them into one of the following two groups—the service-sensitive or the self-service-oriented.

Service-Sensitive. My mother is definitely service-sensitive. She really loved the days of the Sears Catalogue desk with the nice friendly little old ladies behind the counter who were willing to discuss your needs and fill out your order blanks. Now with the new improved computerized system of ordering by touch-tone telephone keyboard, my mother hasn't ordered a single thing from Sears in years. The service-sensitive are those who are willing to pay for the privilege of dealing with a person rather than a machine, of talking to a bank teller rather than keying an ATM. Many people at the university are just like my mother; they would rather call and talk to someone in the IR office than search the electronic or printed fact book. We talk to those people when they call because we want to help them and because they give us valuable information on how to make our *Fact Book* even more user-friendly.

Self-Service-Oriented. At the other end of the continuum are the self-service-oriented. My favorite associate dean, for instance, wants his graphs on a diskette and data sent to him electronically. He is a computer whiz and enjoys utilizing all the capabilities available on the latest and greatest PC hardware and software; a real do-it-yourselfer or self-service type. Although it isn't always true, the distinction on our campus between the service-sensitive and the self-service-oriented generally is determined by the customer's inclination to deal with computers regardless of how user-friendly the system. Consequently, we have found it useful to maintain an office and a fact book that recognize the different styles of the users. To accommodate the university community and the various needs and personalities of the university, we maintain both an electronic fact book and a traditional paper-based fact book format. As noted later in this chapter, the electronic version of the fact book has not replaced the paper fact book but instead offers another mode of presentation and operation. To ensure that the fact book is a valuable resource means that information must be available through a variety of media. Our paper *Fact Book* is still by far the method of choice for all our customers. There is no single information source that is used more. Even the technological whizzes still want their paper copy. And although I haven't quite made the transition to the orthopedic shoes yet, for the service-sensitive I am the old Sears catalogue lady.

Distribution. Distribution is another audience or customer consideration in dealing with the communication of information. Almost every page of our *Fact Book* is distributed campuswide or to a specific audience before the books are actually published. Small reports or single pages of the fact book are circulated during monthly expanded cabinet meetings, weekly cabinet meetings, and the dean's meetings. Other information that I know is of interest to individuals is also distributed as the reports are completed. For example, I send ACT data, retention data, and first-time freshmen information to Recruiting and Admissions as soon as it is done. A faculty member in sociology has an interest in student demographic data, so I forward those fact book pages directly to him at the same time.

Another consideration for distribution is the detail required by different constituencies. My general rule is to send summary data to administrators and send detailed data to department chairs. Administrators have a need for global trends; faculty chairs, for the most part, want information specific to their majors only. Unless otherwise requested or instructed, we send less detail up the ladder and more detail down the ladder. Fact sheets, fact pamphlets, and pocket-sized, abbreviated fact books are most useful to administrators, development officers, alumni directors, and public relations personnel. The detailed breakdowns by major and college, for instance, are of greater use to the people directly involved in the specific programs than to others, so we use the documentation supporting those fact book pages as reports to them.

Eyes Over Forty. One final consideration I insist we make for our audience when producing the fact book and other IR reports is what I call the test for eyes over forty. Television, video, computers, and even *USA Today* have created and cater to a visual environment. Graphs, charts, and figures are beginning to dominate the information scene, and with the technology available, the options for their use are almost endless. It is easy to get carried away with the possibilities. Because most of our users have eyes more than forty years old (particularly the administrators), my rules are no scripty, curvy fonts, small print, or confusing patterns. The chart, graph, or figure passes the test if I don't have to use my glasses to read it.

On the subject of graphs and charts, it is my preference that all graphs and charts in our work answer three questions: Where were we?, Where are we now?, and, Where do we want to be? (Boyett and Conn, 1991). I think such consistency in the graphs and charts helps the reader understand what is being communicated.

Audience-Based Fact Books

In an attempt to meet the contextual considerations influencing the use of our fact book, we publish five fact books of varying sizes, shapes, and descriptions at the University of Southern Mississippi. Although each fact book product meets a particular audience need, each also serves to meet one or more of the fact book purposes I describe later in the chapter.

Fact Sheet. "Quick Facts," as I sometimes call it, is a one-pager officially called the *USM Institutional Profile*. Each fall our first and probably most important institutional research project is to complete the *Institutional Profile*, a single-page fact sheet that is distributed to each employee of the university. Several thousand copies are printed to meet the continuous requests for the *Profile* and its information. This one-page fact sheet is perhaps the most popular and well-used report of any our office publishes. Some offices routinely ask for the *Profile* on diskette and others, like the College of Business, have used the fact-sheet format for their own college fact sheet. The *Profile* fact sheet has also proven to be very useful for speech and grant writers and others who want to boast about the university for the sake of pride as well as profit.

Fact Pamphlet. Our second most widely distributed fact book product is a pamphlet called *Facts and Figures*. Originally we printed 1,000 copies of the pamphlet, but when forced one year into a second printing we increased the initial order. Faculty like to take the fact pamphlet to conferences and the alumni office likes the format for including in their conference packets. I always take one in my own meeting folder and usually end up giving my copy to someone who wants to know more about the university. Public relations officers are big fans and users of the material in this type of format. The fact pamphlet is inexpensive to produce, because it is simply a fold-up version of one-half legal size paper. I was introduced to this fact book format on a visit to the University of Amsterdam, when my Dutch colleague, Liesbeth vanWelie, gave me a fact pamphlet about the University of Amsterdam. In a matter of minutes I knew the number of colleges and students and budget for that institution. It was a fast and convenient way to communicate and it proved to be such a good traveler. Our fact pamphlet contains institutional data for one year on nearly all of the major content areas in our big fact book.

Pocket Fact Book. Our third type of fact book publication is the *USM Pocket Fact Book*. It has a smaller audience than the fact sheet and the fact pamphlet and contains a two-year comparison of institutional data. All upper-level administrators receive a copy of the *Pocket Fact Book*. It too is very popular and the distribution has now increased to about three hundred copies a year. This year the *Pocket Fact Book* went into a second printing because it was sent out with packets mailed to presidential candidates as well as to candidates considered in several other key administrative searches. This publication could have a greater audience were it not for the expense: the size of the pocket fact book is a little odd and therefore more costly to print.

The origin of the USM *Pocket Fact Book* is both interesting and telling. During my first year as director of the institutional research office the president's secretary came to my office with some dogeared index cards with various statistics written on them. She told me that the president carried the index cards in his suit pocket for reference on the road and asked me to update the cards. Not only did that request give me the idea for the pocket fact book, but it also gave me the specific data that the president thought was important enough to have no matter where he was. My first edition of a pocket fact book was typed on a typewriter and cut the size of a pocket. It was an extremely limited edition—there were six copies: one for the president; one for each vice president; and one for me. Numerous requests for the handy little pocket fact book followed, and thanks to desktop publishing a more sophisticated and efficiently produced version followed. The unique value of this document is that in an instant the two-year comparison of institutional data indicates growth or decline in the major areas of institutional performance.

Electronic Fact Book. Although our fact book assessment overwhelmingly indicates that the majority of people on our campus are still more comfortable with the paper format of the fact book than the electronic one, we still recognize the need to keep the technologically literate and self-service data users satisfied with an electronic version. If asked to guess, I would say that as more faculty and staff become comfortable with the technology available and the available technology becomes more friendly, there will be a growing demand for electronic access to fact book data. Although the laptop may never replace the need for a printed fact book, I do think computer access to the data will reduce the number of printed copies we will have to distribute. Part of the information distribution mix is the need for institutional researchers to stay at the cutting edge of electronic data dissemination, and I think maintaining an electronic fact book is one good way to stay current with the technology and its use. We are, after all, in the business of providing information, and that includes using the best available technology and skills to get the job done effectively and efficiently. The USM *Electronic Fact Book* is provided through mainframe access to the Honeywell (that is, The Bull). Users follow a menu system designed by the computing center to get the information they want.

Traditional Paper-Bound Fact Book. By using the word *traditional* to describe this fact book, I intend not only to suggest the typical 8½ by 11 inch printed and bound fact book, but a fact book that is basically reporting one year or more of fall data. Fall data has long been the official reporting data for the university and is still the most important semester of the academic year. However, I have found that for planning purposes administrators and faculty need to know what the other semesters look like as well. So our fact book now gives a snapshot of fall, spring, and summer semester data and, because our departmental budgets are allocated based on student credit hours generated, the fact book has a full academic year of departmental student credit hours by lower, upper, and graduate levels. In order to better use the fact book as a planning and assessment document, I think it should contain some trend data and we have expanded the USM fact book to include whenever possible five years of data to help decipher future trends and, in some cases, to answer productivity kinds of questions. In some areas, *at-a-glance* charts with ten years of data by college, along with university totals, have been added as performance indicators. In addition to the inclusive semester data, trend data, and at-a-glance data previously mentioned, we've added a *everything you've always wanted to know on a single page* feature to our fact book as another way of meeting the needs of frequent and not-so-frequent users in our audience.

This fact book may be traditional in size and shape, but we hope it is establishing new traditions in content and presentation. Like other institutional fact books, ours has evolved from a yearly status quo report into a more historic and dynamic study of the university. But we think the fact book needs to be even more than that.

Purposes and Uses of the Information

Fact books must evolve over time as information needs redefine expectations for data. Once it was enough to know *how many* and *how much,* but the data provided to answer those questions is not necessarily the data needed to answer the questions of *why* and *how well,* and it seems to me that the fact book must speak to the new questions and issues as well. The only tradition we want to preserve for the fact book is one of providing the information our audience needs for their work, and that tradition, I think, is reflected in our ideas of the purposes of fact books.

As I see it, there are ten primary purposes for our fact book products, and although they are certainly not unique to me, my office, or my university, we may view each purpose a little differently than other offices and institutions, and those differences may be reflected in our fact book.

The Fact Book as a Working Document. The fact book is not only an information resource but also an educational tool to teach us all more about our institutions. For example, the glossary of terms in our fact book was developed to define terms in frequently asked questions like "what is a full-time student?," perhaps the most commonly asked question about student data, yet one that is dependent on definitions that aren't always fully understood, as is true of many other questions about institutional issues. By defining the terms and the data, we hope to achieve a better understanding of the data and their use.

Quite simply, the first and most important purpose of the fact book is as a tool: something to use when information and data are needed to understand, explain, plan, decide, evaluate, assess, or accomplish a host of other individual or institutional tasks. And, to accomplish these tasks, I think the fact book needs to meet the following purposes as well.

Historical Record of the University. "Rational types focus on facts and facts are about the past" (Davis, 1987, p. 222). Studying an institution's past can increase the likelihood of facing the challenges of a quickly changing present and unknown future with strategic forethought. Information-based decisions can begin with studying the fact book for historical perspective. Given that the average university president's tenure at any given institution is no longer than five years, it is certain that the president will have a need to learn something about the history of the institution and the current performance of the institution from some factual concise document like a fact book. Because I do not find a number meaningful in isolation, I always try to include trend information, comparison information, or some sort of time line in the fact book to provide historical perspective. The practical reality is that the fact book is the only place on campus where significant institutional data are consistently maintained over time.

Public Relations (Internal and External). Fact books can be used for both internal public relations and for external press releases. Many times I fax a fact book page or two to a journalist hoping that the printed information will be better understood (copied) than the spoken word, and knowing from experience that the printed material will provoke better questions than a telephone interview. The fact book should represent the status of the institution, answer questions about the university's mission, and give a general description of the students and faculty at the university. The office of public relations receives at least thirty fact books each year. All PR personnel receive a copy, and the PR officers also distribute the fact books to the local press so that they have a professional and official reference for their newspaper stories. Perhaps the real practical value of the fact book in public relations is that the same answers are generally available no matter who is asking the questions or who is answering.

Planning and Decision Making. Although there are, and most likely always will be, plans and decisions made in higher education not based on data, the preponderance of decisions are data based. Plans are generally based on some knowledge of where the institution has been, where it is now, and projections of where it might be going, and that knowledge is most often rooted in the data and information provided in the fact book: if the planning data are not in the fact book, they should be. If, as Larry Jones keeps trying to tell me, every decision represents a plan of some kind or another, the outcome of that plan can be judged at some future point in time. However subtle, data usually provide the means for evaluating plans and decisions, and whether it is data on the students, faculty, programs, or general operations of the institution, the fact book provides the basic source of information to evaluate what the institution is trying to do and what it is accomplishing. The fact book should provide data that will help monitor the planning and decision processes.

Institutional Effectiveness. The fact book provides institutional effectiveness information in basically two areas: input data and output data. Input data, such as admission test scores on admitted and enrolled students, student characteristics and demographics, and the numbers of students enrolled in programs, provide good baseline information to the departments about the preparation and quality of students, where they come from and their background, and what they may need from the program. Output data include grade point averages, retention, persistence and graduation information and degrees awarded. A fact book can and should provide most of the documentation for the accreditation process or other accountability measures, including data and information directly tied to performance indicators that have recently found their way into the literature and institutional operations.

Performance Indicators. Performance indicators are important factors in planning for the future and for budgeting purposes. Performance indicators fall into basically three categories: trend studies, workload studies, and cost efficiency studies. Legislators and the public have a great interest in performance indicator information because they believe it will help them understand the relationship between increasing costs and productivity, as measured by numbers of graduates and faculty workload, to name just two popular indicators. I have included and expanded performance indicator baseline data into five-year trend information in the electronic fact book, although the same information could be calculated from data in the printed fact book. The purpose is to provide the data so that those interested in doing the analyses on performance indicators have it readily available.

Self-Study and Accreditation. In 1995, the University of Southern Mississippi completed the reaffirmation self-study process. That year the production and distribution of the *Fact Book* increased by nearly three hundred copies. All the faculty members who were members of the self-study committee received fact books to begin their personal studies of the institution. All members of the accreditation visiting team received copies of the *Fact Book* before arriving on campus. Many of the self-study committee reports included *Fact Book* data and information. The self-study document included an introduction taken directly from the *Fact Book* and *Fact Book* graphics and tables, which were not only useful in writing the report but which the visiting team reported were particularly valuable in speeding up the reading process. The self-study director, an English professor, said that neither he nor the committees could improve on the fact book information used in the deliberations or the reporting. That alone was motivation to keep up a fact book reporting process, which can at times get tedious, and to keep working at making the *Fact Book* a vital part of the institution.

Grant Proposals, Research Projects, and Development Activities. When I first arrived in institutional research as a research assistant, I received a visit from a grants officer on campus for some information. Trying to be my wonderful, helpful self, I actually filled in the grant information for her. I soon learned that I was so convenient that she brought me more and more grant proposals to complete. Well, my second fall semester I was ready for her visit, but this time I gave her a personal copy of the *Fact Book* so she could fill out her own reports. I have been sending multiple copies to grants officers ever since. The *Fact Book* saves us both tremendous amounts of time.

Orientation for New Employees. Recently our university has completed a presidential search, and, of course, the *Fact Book* was one of the major documents sent to the perspective candidates. I was very pleased when one of the presidential candidates repeatedly referred to the *Fact Book* in his presentations to the faculty, deans, and cabinet. He actually said that one could learn a little about the entire university from that single document and he thanked me personally for the information. Other new employees find their way to my office to request the *Fact Book,* particularly those people in public relations, administrative, and fundraising positions. Not only do we help the newcomers, but we establish early friendships with colleagues whom we later often have to call on for help.

Legal Documentation. Institutional Research and Planning is located next door to University Legal Counsel. I am not sure that it was intentional but a result has been frequent visits from the university attorney to obtain legal documentation. First, I gave him a current USM *Fact Book,* which he found very useful, then discovered he had copied the last twenty years of *Fact Books* because much of the litigation is from past years. On a less formal and less official basis, we also serve the clients from legal services, as they find their way in for copies of the fact book. We supply the fact book when requested, but don't offer advice, legal or otherwise, even if asked: we have learned something from being next door to the legal counsel. The fact book is, of course, a public record that is used by both plaintiffs and defendants.

CFBI: Continuous Fact Book Improvement

"A man was looking on the ground for his lost key. When his neighbor asked him where he lost it, he pointed to a different place. 'Then why aren't you looking there?' asked the neighbor. The man replied, 'Because the light is better here'" (Hoca, 1987). The institutional researcher's role is to make the light better in the fact book. To make certain we have the light in the right place and shining on the data and information our colleagues are seeking, we include a written evaluation form in each fact book (Exhibit 6.1) and conduct a telephone survey and personal interviews every three years. The evaluation forms and the surveys and interviews have given us positive and useful feedback for improving our fact book, and we are happy to have it as we continue to develop our fact book products. We have also found it helpful to read and evaluate fact books from other institutions and, when appropriate, to borrow ideas we think would work for us: we hope others are using our fact book when they can to improve their own.

Perhaps the easiest way to summarize my strategies for making the fact book work is to paraphrase the idea of mass customizing (Davis, 1987) and Sally's *I want it like I want it* philosophy: my goal is mass personalization. I really do want it like they want it.

Exhibit 6.1. USM Fact Book Evaluation Form

The Office of Institutional Planning and Analysis is committed to providing quality information services to the university community. Please assist us by answering the following questions and returning this page to our office; you may simply clip the page, fold it, and send it through campus mail. Your assessment will be important to us as we prepare next year's FACTBOOK and numerous other reports and publications.

	Needs Improvement				Excellent
Comprehensiveness of information	1	2	3	4	5
Organization of information	1	2	3	4	5
Usefulness of information	1	2	3	4	5
Legibility of format	1	2	3	4	5
Clarity of graphics	1	2	3	4	5
Overall quality of FACTBOOK	1	2	3	4	5

Is there additional information that you would like to see included in future editions of the FACTBOOK? If so, please specify:

Is there information which you believe could be eliminated from future editions of the FACTBOOK? If so, please specify:

How often do you refer to the FACTBOOK?

Please offer any suggestions for improvement:

References

Boyett, J., and Conn, H. *Workplace 2000: The Revolution Reshaping American Business.* New York: Penguin, 1991.

Davis, S. *Future Perfect.* New York: Addison-Wesley, 1987.

Hoca, N. Quoted in S. Davis, *Future Perfect.* New York: Addison-Wesley, 1987, p. 192.

Valery, P. Quoted in S. Davis, *Future Perfect.* New York: Addison-Wesley, 1987, p. 10.

ANN W. TOMLINSON *is director of institutional planning and analysis at the University of Southern Mississippi.*

The fact book is a tool for improving the processes and products of higher education.

The Fact Book: A Tool for Institutional Improvement

Larry G. Jones

In the James Burke television series called *Connections* (1978), significant contemporary phenomena are analyzed through an examination of events seemingly unrelated by time and space using some commonplace item or event as the vehicle of exploration. In the several episodes that I have watched, I have been impressed by how simple most complex things can be made to seem, and by how complex some seemingly simple things are in reality; by how discovery is probably more a serendipitous result than one of inspiration or perspiration; how important unintended consequences are in the course of human events; and how often the creative idea is built on the perceived failure of some other concept. These same generalizations seem to fit the ongoing development of higher education as well as events and issues on most college and university campuses. I think they also describe the conceptual development and use of the institutional fact book as a primary source of and for institutional knowledge.

Borrowing from the program format of *Connections,* my purpose is to show how the institutional fact book, as simple a research document as it may seem, has come to fulfill four significant objectives in the process of institutional study; objectives which, I believe, evolve from the relationship between the study of higher education and institutional research (as seemingly unrelated by time and space as those two sometimes appear) and from the influence (or lack thereof) the study of higher education and institutional research have had on higher education. The connection between the institutional fact book, institutional research, and the study of higher education will become clear, I hope, as the themes develop: at least that is the way it works on the television program.

NEW DIRECTIONS FOR INSTITUTIONAL RESEARCH, no. 91, Fall 1996 © Jossey-Bass Publishers

The basic premise of this chapter is that the fact book is, or could become, the single most important document published by any institution of higher education. My conclusion is based on the following four theses: the fact book presents tangible evidence, and often the only public evidence, that an institution is open to the systematic study and review of its programs, processes, and outcomes by its constituents; the fact book provides, and is often the only source of institutional data required by constituents to fulfill their responsibilities and obligations and to increase their knowledge and understanding of institutional mission and effectiveness; the fact book provides a basis for internal and external evaluation and assessment of the institution's mission, goals, priorities, accomplishments, and effectiveness; and the ongoing qualitative and quantitative development of the fact book directly reflects the success or failure of the institution to keep pace with the educational, sociological, and technological opportunities of the near and mid-range future. Now for the connections and the defense of the premise and the theses.

Premise: the fact book is, or could become, the single most important document published by an institution. There are, of course, other important publications issued regularly or irregularly by colleges and universities, but who would argue that a college catalog is really offered to the public for the purpose of systematic study of institutional operation. In fact, college catalogs are notorious more for their prose (fiction) than for their fact. Faculty registers or directories are interesting data sources for some research on faculty, but hardly a source for more comprehensive study of faculty or the institution. President's reports, alumni publications, admissions material, and student handbooks all make interesting reading, but hardly the material researchers turn to for the substance to write an institutional self-study, to document a long-range plan, or to provide evidence of institutional effectiveness. Institutional histories generally prove that a scholarly examination of institutional history can be a valuable frame of reference, but more immediate quantitative and qualitative help is needed if the institution is to look better in the next revision or volume of institutional history.

By providing significant and substantial institutional data, the institutional fact book becomes not only the source of data for institutional study and review, but the symbolic inspiration for institutional progress by featuring and documenting institutional accomplishment. In other words, the fact book is probably the only manual, guidebook, or handbook available to the institution for critical self-study, and is clearly the major resource for hard evidence related to institutional mission. If it is not, perhaps we need to ask, why not?

Thesis one: The fact book presents tangible evidence, and often the only public evidence, that an institution is open to the systematic study and review of its programs, processes, and outcomes by its constituents. Although it may seem to many college and university faculty members and administrators that colleges and universities spend too much of their time studying, reviewing, evaluating, and pondering the work of the institution, other interested publics wonder if anybody on campus knows what is going on.

These opposing views are exacerbated in part because the general public usually only sees and reads the more critical analyses of life on college and university campuses, and in part because much of the research on higher education is not written or presented in a fashion that is of interest to the public, and even some faculty for that matter.

Although we all know good institutional research is conducted on campus, we don't present a lot of evidence to show that it is being used, or that it is having any benefit. The problem is that most institutional research never sees the light of day, and most faculty never know the studies are even done. In the mean time, the public, the popular media, the *Chronicle of Higher Education,* the professional journals, the legislature, the parents of our students, and an increasing number of disgruntled students and faculty are asking serious questions about what we are doing and how well we are doing it.

Into this environment of not-so-quiet skepticism over what we know about what we are doing comes the fact book, a simple compilation of significant data and information that signals someone is paying attention. If nothing else, the fact book says to those who are wondering just what is going on, here are the data: now you know what we know: help us figure it out. The fact book begs the question of what all of this means to me and thee, and what can we do about it.

My concern, however, is not so much with the quality or quantity of the institutional research as much as it is with the fact that there are so few who seem to know what to study or why. I worry about administrators and faculty writing assessment and outcomes measures who think Bloom's Taxonomy is a plant book. I get concerned when administrators can list the tenets of TQM (Total Quality Management) and CQI (Continuous Quality Improvement) but have trouble identifying the concepts of Pat Cross's classroom research or Alexander Astin's assessment model. Does Demming make institutional sense if you don't know what Pascarella and Terenzini have to say? Who are Frederick Rudolph and T. R. McConnel and Paul Dressel and Howard Bowen and Algo Henderson and Wilbert McKeachie? And what did they know anyhow? Is higher education the only profession where there are virtually no entry requirements demanding some demonstrable understanding of basic processes (learning and teaching in this case) or historical and institutional environments? There was a moment in time, in fact about the time most higher education programs were started, when it was thought we could teach and train professional administrators to manage the growth of colleges and universities. As it turned out, faculty selection committees were unimpressed by the importance of academic preparation in higher education administration when it came to administering academic programs or institutions.

So, how does this connect to the fact book and the study of institutions of higher education and the institutional research conducted to review mission, programs, and outcomes of a specific institution? Well, as it turns out, the fact book is not a bad text book for the in-service and continuing education for faculty and administrators. And, whatever else might be said about college faculty or administrators, they are not stupid. Give them the consequences of a few more tight budget years and, armed with fact book data, they will find the right questions to ask and the appropriate references to document their findings, conclusions, and recommendations. The same fact book data are equally useful in answering the probing questions of legislators, reporters, and others interested in knowing more about institutions and higher education, and, more important, those interested in wanting to know what institutions know about what they are doing. Perhaps all fact books should include a bibliography or list of selected references for each section to connect institutional research to the research on higher education. That connects to the second thesis.

Thesis two: The fact book provides, and is often the only source of institutional data required by constituents to fulfill their responsibilities and obligations and increase their knowledge and understanding of institutional mission and effectiveness. One could argue that there has been a conspiracy to limit access to institutional data because someone didn't want others to know what they knew. Information is power in most situations, and we might argue that there are some in power who simply don't want others to know, or to even ask the questions. At one of the better private liberal arts colleges, the president refused to release one year's fact book after it had been published for fear of what would be known. According to another reliable source, the first fact book at a major research university was in the process of being numbered and coded for secure distribution to the *inner circle* when the president walked in and suggested that the fact book be given to all faculty and staff.

Although fact books have made access to institutional data much easier, there still persists on some campuses, even with fact books, the notion that some campus information is not for everyone. At one major research university, a senior associate vice president was routinely questioned about how data he requested would be used, and whether or not he needed what he was asking for to do his job. It seems strange that at an institution aspiring to be one of the top ten teaching, research, and service institutions in the country, where faculty and researchers routinely manage research for which they are given grants and contracts totaling millions of dollars, that someone somewhere is wondering whether administrators and faculty can handle institutional data not in their chosen area of expertise. Imagine what would happen if a librarian told mathematicians they could not check out philosophy books because the concepts, ideas, and information were not in their area of expertise. Some administrators and faculty have found it easier to obtain information for evaluating their programs from other institutions than to obtain the same data from their own campus. It all sounds preposterous, but it is true nevertheless.

Rather than attribute the lack of data access entirely to misguided human judgment, it might be better to lay some of the access problem at the feet of technology. In the old days of main frame computers run by punch cards and punch-card-eating machinery, data were not so easily accessed. The fact book took data from the green bar paper, put it in a presentable format, and made it available to the common person. Since that time, however, technology has put the computer and data on the common person's desk, often right next to the fact book, which hasn't changed much in style or format over the last quarter of a century. But because institutional data still isn't generally available to PC users, the fact book remains the single most important resource for the institutional data required for most campus planning and analysis.

The connection: The Chisholm Trail is to the interstate highway system what the fact book is to the information highway. The fact book was the first significant effort, and in some cases remains the only effort, to provide institutional data to those who can use it. Just as the *roads* have improved so have the *vehicles* used to travel them. Perhaps more important, the fact book reaffirms the notion that information is not only power but it is also the most important product provided by higher education.

Thesis three: The fact book directly and indirectly provides a basis for internal and external evaluation and assessment of the institution's mission, goals, priorities, accomplishments, and effectiveness. The fact book connection with internal and external evaluation, assessment, or accountability is clearly built on the first two theses. Whatever else may be said about making comparisons or judgments about the institution based on fact book data, the only certain thing is that it beats using the manufactured institutional data offered in the best-selling ratings issues of *Money, U.S. News and World Report,* and the other publications making big bucks providing an unsuspecting public with what is purported to be meaningful analysis. At some point in time, and perhaps it would be good to debate the merits of the move before it happens, institutional fact books will provide common data in common formats to provide richer analysis for those wishing to do comparisons with peers. The IPEDS (Integrated Postsecondary Education Data Survey) reporting project of the National Center for Education Statistics must be viewed as a step in this direction, as must the cooperative data exchanges of the Southern University Group (SUG), the Association of American Universities (AAUDE), Higher Education Data System (HEDS), and the College Information Systems Association (CISA). One might also assume that Student Right-To-Know legislation, required NCAA reporting, and the *trigger* concept incorporated in the stillborn SPRE (State Postsecondary Review Entity) guidelines will simply take institutional data and reporting further down this potholed stretch of the information highway.

In his course in institutional research at the University of Georgia, Pat Terenzini taught the importance of unobtrusive measures available for institutional research, and like Terenzini, I believe the fact book is one of the best sources of such data available. For instance, the institution that has made diversity a priority had better have race and sex data in the fact book, and there had better be supporting evidence to document the accomplishment of institutional mission and goals. What data and information the institution chooses to report and how it chooses to report it can say more about institutional quality than the data itself and certainly more than any public relations effort will ever be able communicate. Equally important in these unobtrusive measures is the fact book itself. Like all institutional publications fact book appearance is important but, as we all know, one doesn't judge a book by its cover. A slick publication filled with colorful pictures, fancy figures, and animated tables may be attractive to the eye, but making a fact book serve as an institutional infomercial is likely to meet with the same acceptance by constituents as a classic comic might with the comparative literature faculty. A fact book can be a good public relations tool, but public relations shouldn't be the only purpose of a fact book.

The fact book connection with institutional evaluation is most clearly illustrated by its use in the accreditation process. In the Southern Association of Colleges and Schools (SACS) region, the institutional fact book is a frequently used supplement to the institutional self-study. In fact, during recent discussions in the revision of the SACS *Criteria for Accreditation,* consideration was given to including the fact book, by name, as one of the functions of institutional research. The institutional research functions are included in the section on institutional effectiveness in the *Criteria,* and they include most of the purposes and objectives ascribed to fact books (Southern Association of Colleges and Schools, 1995).

Thesis four: The ongoing qualitative and quantitative development of the fact book directly reflects the success or failure of the institution in keeping pace with the educational, sociological, and technological opportunities of the new and mid-range future. The fourth thesis does not necessarily describe a cause and effect relationship, but there will be a strong correlation between institutions recognized among the best and institutions which have made the most of fact book data connections to their mission and goals. Let me connect the premise and the theses by proposing a few initiatives focusing on the fact book.

In my first thesis, I suggest that the fact book is the instigator of institutional research as well as a repository of institutional research. Using the fact book as a text book, institutions have the means, and an implied obligation, to educate administrators, students, faculty, and all interested constituents about important institutional issues. My real intent, however, is to make all faculty and staff institutional researchers. Not only do we need more institutional research, but we need more people doing institutional research if we are to meet internal and external information needs. And we clearly need a more literate higher education faculty if we are to meet institutional goals and objectives. I think the *fact book as text book* concept can provide the connection. Every institution should charge someone with the responsibility for seeing that this continuing higher education is available: this may or may not be one of the formal institutional research functions. Institutions that find new ways and vehicles to involve more faculty, and a more knowledgeable faculty, in more institutional management will likely be the leading institutions of the future.

Technological advances already make it possible to provide institutional data in far more user-friendly fashion than hard copy fact books, and in fact, electronic fact books are in place at some institutions. Future fact books may take the form of fact book *floppies,* formatted disks that allow administrators or faculty members the opportunity to make their own fact book pages and do their own fact book analyses. Picture the committee meeting of tomorrow, when faculty use their laptop computers to obtain the essential data for committee decisions from a Web site or links to other institutional or educational data. Perhaps the question is whether or not institutions can survive an age when faculty committees take less than an academic year to reach closure.

Finally, the fact book connection with institutional evaluation is paramount. If we, as faculty, administrators, and researchers do not provide the leadership in establishing the appropriate data and analysis for evaluation, assessment, and accountability, we will never overcome the misinformation damage done by publishers of institutional ratings, by legislators setting reporting requirements, or even by the NCAA, which by default has become the repository of national graduation and retention data. The fact book concept is the means by which institutions provide and connect the appropriate data and the contextual analysis for institutional evaluation.

When I edited the *University of Georgia Fact Book,* I was often annoyed by the suggestion that the fact book was all I did. I have since come to realize that it was the most important thing I did. The fact book not only constitutes the most important institutional research the institution needs, it also connects the research to everything the institution does.

References

Burke, J. *Connections: An Alternative View of Change.* British Broadcasting Corporation, 1978.
Southern Association of Colleges and Schools. *Criteria for Accreditation.* Decatur, Ga.: Southern Association of Colleges and Schools, Commission on Colleges, 1995.

LARRY G. JONES is public service associate and associate professor in the Institute of Higher Education at the University of Georgia.

INDEX

Accountability. *See* Campus fact books: and accountability issues

Adler, M., 37

Andrews, G., 18

Astin, A., 91

Axt, R. G., 7

Banta, T., 41

"Being digital," 63

Bluhm, H. P., 12

Boggs, J. R., 13

Bogue, G., 28

Borden, V., 41

Bowen, H., 91

Boyett, J., 79, 81

Brinkman, P., 41

Browne, M. N., 37

Burkan, W. C., 67

Burke, J., 89

Campus fact books: and accountability issues, 28; as assessment tool, 93–94; bias in, 45; as catalogs for specific reports, 29; cost to produce, 15; data management in, 11, 13, 17; detail, level of, 37; development, 35; distribution of, 15; as empowerment tools, 14; evaluation form, sample, 88; as evidence of self-study, 90–92; *Fact Book for Academic Administrators,* 9; *Fact Book for the Florida State University,* 10; *Fact Book on Higher Education,* 9; *Fact Book on Higher Education in the South,* 3–5; *Fact Book on Western Higher Education,* 7; *Facts About New England Colleges and Universities,* 7; format of, 16, 43; foundations, 27; future of, 24; general purpose, 36–37; as historical record, 84–85; history of, 1, 3–24; illustrated, 31; importance of, 12, 92; improving, 30–33, 78; information, accuracy of, 43; information in, 42; information, presentation of, 43; for institutional effectiveness, 85–86; intranet, distribution by, 14; issues-oriented, 36, 41; items in, 38–41; as labor-saving device, 13; memory-facilitating techniques and, 44; mini fact book, 16, 82–83; and mission statement, 37; as most important document of institution, 90; obsolescence of, 28–29; organization of, 52–54; and performance indicators, 86; popularity of, growth in, 12; physical appearance, 44; production considerations, 36; for public relations, 85; as reaction to higher education conditions, 7; reasons for not publishing, 13–15; regional data in, need for, 7; sample goal questions, 36; shortcomings of, 30–31; specialized, 16–17; as textbook, 94; thoroughness of, 36; and total quality management, 14; types of, 27–28; as working document, 84. *See also* Electronic fact books; Fact book audience issues; Fact book content development; Fact book as institutional research report; Fact book layout and design; Fact book textual concerns; Fact book uses; Fact book variants

Carter, E., 13

Conn, H., 79, 81

Connections, 89

Continuous quality improvement (CQI), 91

Creech, J., 28

Cross, P., 91

Daly, R. F., 2, 14, 16, 20, 22, 43, 63, 65

Data: confidentiality of, 14, 45, 92; ethical treatment of, 45; shared, dangers of, 14, 45, 92

Davis, S., 79, 80, 84, 87

Desktop publishing (DTP), 49–59

Deming, W. E., 91

Dressel, P., 91

Eck, J. 11

Electronic fact books: advantages of, 66–67; availability of, 68; characteristics, 67–69; creating, in seven days, 72–74; data format of, 67; as decision support tool, 66; drill-down capabilities, 65, 67; examples, locations of, 64; flat-file, 65, 68; functions of, 65–66; implementation readiness, 69–71; impracticality of, 92–93; as management reporting tool, 66; as marketing

ORDERING INFORMATION

NEW DIRECTIONS FOR INSTITUTIONAL RESEARCH is a series of paperback books that provides planners and administrators in all types of academic institutions with guidelines in such areas as resource coordination, information analysis, program evaluation, and institutional management. Books in the series are published quarterly in spring, summer, fall, and winter and are available for purchase by subscription as well as by single copy.

SUBSCRIPTIONS cost $52.00 for individuals (a savings of 35 percent over single-copy prices) and $79.00 for institutions, agencies, and libraries. Please do not send institutional checks for personal subscriptions. Standing orders are accepted.

SINGLE COPIES cost $20.00 plus shipping (see below) when payment accompanies order. California, New Jersey, New York, and Washington, D.C., residents please include appropriate sales tax. Canadian residents add GST and any local taxes. Billed orders will be charged shipping and handling. No billed shipments to post office boxes. Orders from outside the United States or Canada *must be prepaid* in U.S. dollars or charged to VISA, MasterCard, or American Express.

SHIPPING (SINGLE COPIES ONLY): $10.00 and under, add $2.50; $10.01–$20, add $3.50; $20.01–$50, add $4.50; $50.01–$75, add $5.50; $75.01–$100, add $6.50; $100.01–$150, add $7.50; over $150, add $8.50. Outside of North America, please add $15.00 per book for priority shipment.

DISCOUNTS FOR QUANTITY ORDERS are available. Please write to the address below for information.

ALL ORDERS must include either the name of an individual or an official purchase order number. Please submit your order as follows:
   Subscriptions: specify series and year subscription is to begin
   Single copies: include individual title code (such as IR78)

MAIL ALL ORDERS TO:
   Jossey-Bass Publishers
   350 Sansome Street
   San Francisco, CA 94104-1342

FOR SUBSCRIPTION SALES OUTSIDE OF THE UNITED STATES, CONTACT:
any international subscription agency or Jossey-Bass directly.